# The Making of a Winner

## by David E. Moe

Winning Ways Press
Issaquah, WA 98027

Other book by David E. Moe:
OPENING HEARTS AND MINDS

Library of Congress
Catalog Card Number: 87-090413

ISBN: 0-9615797-1-4

Published by Winning Ways Press
12900 246th S.E.
Issaquah, WA 98057

Printed and bound in the United States of America.

# TABLE OF CONTENTS

Chapter  1 - Frustration                                    1

Chapter  2 - Suck On That One                               5

Chapter  3 - Tennis On The Mind                            15

Chapter  4 - Morning Lesson                                23

Chapter  5 - Volition                                      39

Chapter  6 - Movies Of The Mind                            51

Chapter  7 - Tennis Date                                   61

Chapter  8 - Math Olympiad                                 71

Chapter  9 - Another Lesson                                79

Chapter 10 - Marlene's Gift                                89

Chapter 11 - Tournament                                    95

Chapter 12 - Finals                                       101

                Epilogue                                  108

                Recommended Readings                      110

# DEDICATION

I would like to dedicate this book to my two sons, Michael and Steven. I wish them the best Life has to offer.

# "CAUTION"

As you read this book remember to treat yourself with the kindness and understanding that you would give a friend. The wisdom contained herein can be of greater benefit if allowed to be assimilated on a gradual basis. Take what you find useful and feel no pressure to use everything you read here. This book was written for all who wish to create excellence in their lives. It is a road map to find and bring out the excellence within ourselves. May all of Life's best be yours.

*THE ROAD metaphor again.*

*Find the excellence within And bring it forth . EDUCARE*

# ACKNOWLEDGEMENTS

I am deeply indebted to many people who helped me in the creation of this book. Cliff Harvey, Cindy Wignot, and Kay West did the final editing and gave me the last bit of encouragement I needed to finish this project. Renee Watkins created the illustrations and provided editing expertise. Also, Bob Sheedy, Dick Doane, Eric Rush, Courtney Johnston, Earle Irvine, Greg Olson, Jack Estes, John Stoor, James Bennett, Scott Sherman, James Loehr, Arthur Ashe, Patrica Pratt, K.C. Winters read the manuscript and gave valuable feedback. There may be some others whom I have forgotten because this project has taken four years, but I wish to thank them at this time. A very special thanks to Velma Peace who read my first book and was so enthusiastic about it she would not let me sleep until I finished this one. I am going to return the favor to her by insisting that she publish her work.

# Circle of Champions

NEGATIVE EMOTIONS -
    ANGER
    FRUSTRATION
    SELF-DOUBT


MENTAL SKILLS - IMAGINATION - TO IMAGE

SPIRITUAL SKILLS - (BELIEFS) POWER OF BELIEFS

# INTRODUCTION

I wrote this book to help young and old who are learning the game of tennis. After playing the game for over twenty years I finally became enlightened to what the game is all about, i.e. how the mental side of the game works and why the outcome of a match is often determined before the two players step on the court. The Greeks looked on athletics as a means to cultivate the integration of mind, body, and spirit. Modern psychologists might look at it as an arena to discover how our subconscious mind controls what we become.

William James, one of the fathers of twentieth-century psychology, said that the greatest discovery of the nineteenth century was not in the realm of physical science, but in the power of the subconscious mind *tinged* by faith. The faculties of imagination and belief remain the least known and least used of all mental faculties. Yet they are also the most powerful. The story the **Making of a Winner** is about a young boy who has trouble with anger, frustration, and self-doubt on the tennis court. The boy finds a mentor who is able to teach him some spiritual truths and mental skills to overcome these negative emotions and become a better tennis player and person.

All of the people in the book are different parts of me or others I have known. I have taken the liberty to design the characters to fit the story. The sequence of events are real to me. My subconscious sometimes gets carried away with the significance of small events, but always has a spiritual message if I take the time to listen.

Mr. Lovano, the main character in my first book, **Opening Hearts and Minds,** returns in this book to share his wisdom and thoughts as he helps a young boy learn new skills for living and playing the game.

# 1

# FRUSTRATION

WAP! The ball slammed into the net. During the pause before the next serve, John clenched his jaw and tightened his grip on the racket. The second serve floated over the net, a slow blooper that bounced in the middle of the service box, an invitation for John to slam it back at his opponent. Moving up to the ball, John swung at it violently, as if to tear its cover off. The return rocketed into the tape at the top of the net. Raising his hands and looking up in disbelief he cursed and threw his racket into the net. "Nothing is going right," he thought to himself. Stalling for time, he kicked at something on the court and slowly walked to the net to pick up his racket. Reluctantly, positioning himself at the baseline, John waited. The next serve was a high looping shot that floated to the backhand side. Attacking the ball wildly he hit it into the next court.

5-1 in the second set; John was faced with the awesome challenge of two consecutive match points. Receiving another soft serve to the forehand, John lashed out at the ball wildly and sent it sailing over the high chain link fence. Half crying and thoroughly dejected, he stormed out of the gate toward his parents.

"I HATE this game! I HATE it!" He threw his racket down and started for the car.

"John, come back and pick up your racket!" his mother insisted strongly.

"I don't know if I'll need it anymore! I'm NOT good enough to play tennis," he said as he grudgingly picked up the racket.

"Don't you want to watch any more of the matches?" his father asked.

"No Dad, I just want to get away from here," John said impatiently.

They rode home in the car in an uncomfortable silence until John blurted out, "I can't believe how I tense up and miss easy shots! Pete just kept hitting back those balloon balls, never taking any chances. God, how I hate to lose to dinkers. I know I'm a better player than he is. Jeeze, I see those easy shots coming across the net and I want to drill it back at him so hard that he'll never dink the ball over again, but then I blow it, hitting the ball long or into the net."

"Don't get so worked up over it. It's only a game," his mother said as she tried to comfort him.

The car bumped over the curb and stopped in the driveway.

"Oh, Mom you don't understand! You don't understand!" He got out of the car, slammed the door, and headed for the house.

"We are going to have to do something about his temper or he is going to have trouble all his life. You're his father -why don't you do something about it?" said Mrs. Brasky.

"He really tries hard, but he just doesn't know how to handle himself on the tennis court. I'd like to help him, but I don't have the tennis skills."

"Maybe we should spend some money on private lessons. He really needs something," John's mother responded.

"I've been thinking about that also. I wonder how many tennis pros are listed in the phone book," Mr. Brasky said as he opened the car door for his wife. "I think I'll take a look."

"We are going to need a very special kind of person, someone who knows more than just how to swing a tennis racket. I wonder how much lessons would cost?" he thought as he picked up the phone book. He ran his finger through the book to the "T" in the yellow pages. "There are four places listed that give tennis instruction. How do we decide which one? I don't want just any old person or just some young kid. We need someone who understands people and can help John with his feelings and temper. Here's an interesting ad."

"This guy does everything: tennis lessons, biofeedback (whatever that is), sports psychology, and self-esteem. Sports Psychology. Now that sounds like maybe he could help John. Look at his credentials: PH.D. from the School of Hard Knocks! Looks like this guy has a variety of experiences. Well, it can't hurt to call this Mr. Lovano and find out what he is all about. I think I'll do it now while I'm thinking about it."

He dialed the phone. After three rings a recorded message interrupted. Mr. Brasky left a message.

# 2

# SUCK ON THAT ONE

**Imagination is more important than knowledge.**

Albert Einstein.

Mr. Lovano had called back and arranged to meet with John, John's father, and one of John's tennis friends on Saturday morning. Mr. Lovano wanted to observe John playing with someone his age.

It did not take them long to get to the courts, since the courts were located a mile from John's house. Arriving early they would be able to see Mr. Lovano and a friend playing a doubles match with a husband/wife team from out of town. Many people were standing around talking and laughing as they waited for a free court. Mr. Lovano's instructions were to look for a person wearing a dark blue tennis shirt with a light blue collar. He would be playing with a friend who was a Sikh and would be wearing a white turban. John spotted them playing on the end court.

Experience          Books etc.

I can have
*knowledge*

Puts it to
use

But my *imagination* is
what gives knowledge
purpose.

Fig. 1

It was interesting to watch as Mr. Lovano and his Sikh friend played. They seemed to move in harmony with each other. The mixed doubles team was putting up a good battle. It was apparent that the woman was the stronger of the two players. She was quite aggressive and hit the ball very well.

The woman was serving to Mr. Lovano in the deuce court. She had a strong serve. Mr. Lovano glided up to the ball, hit a solid return deep to her forehand, and took a few steps forward moving his way to the net. She acted offended by his confidence and drilled one back at him. Mr. Lovano volleyed the ball to the male opponent near the net. He missed.

As the game progressed she seemed to try anything she could to brush Mr. Lovano off the net and destroy his confidence. During a later point when she was serving to Mr. Lovano's partner, he returned a short ball to her. Since Mr. Lovano was positioned halfway between the baseline and net she tried to put the ball through his navel. He volleyed it deep to her side of the court in the corner and Lovano's team won the point.

The teams traded games back and forth as the set progressed. Later in the set, a similar situation came up where Mr. Lovano's partner hit a ball short to the woman player. Taking advantage of the setup, she moved in for an easy shot. Swinging very deliberately, she again tried to drill it through Mr. Lovano's navel. He was ready and crouched low to volley it, since the ball was sailing low to the net. The ball hit the net and jumped into a trajectory path a foot higher than Mr. Lovano had anticipated. He missed the ball and they lost the point.

"SUCK ON THAT ONE!" she yelled across the net.

She seemed to get a charge out of what had happened and decided to use the incident for all it was worth.

Mr. Lovano stopped still in his tracks and seemed amused at what he had heard. It wasn't what you would have expected from an opponent.

He replayed the shot, acting out hitting the stroke perfectly as if he had made the most beautiful backhand volley deep to his opponent's corner. Then he took a deep breath and relaxed as if he had done something that gave him great joy. The imaginary shot seemed more real to him than the one he missed.

The game continued competitively, but Lovano's team was ahead five games to four and it was match point. Mr. Lovano's partner again hit a weak shot to the aggressive lady opponent. Again the ball was drilled right at Lovano. Confidently he put it away for the game and match point.

John and his father waved to him as he left the court and started walking toward them.

"Nice shot. It was a fun match to watch. That woman was really a tiger," John's dad exclaimed.

"Thanks. You must be Mr. Brasky and this must be John. Glad to meet you."

"This is John's practice partner, Steve."

"Hi Steve! I appreciate your coming along," Mr. Lovano said as he reached out to shake hands.

"I like the way you handled the woman trying to psych you out and work on your confidence. I would like to understand how to maintain such control on the court. Wouldn't you John?" Mr. Brasky broke in. "Maybe Mr. Lovano will share his technique."

"Yeah, I guess so," responded John.

"Well, it depends on what you suck on. Remember the shot the lady hit at me which bounced off the top of the net and I missed. She told me to '**SUCK ON THAT ONE!**' I didn't want to be left remembering myself missing important volleys at the net. So I restroked the shot, imitating the correct movement as vividly as possible. In my mind's eye, I saw the ball land perfectly in the corner. Then I exhaled to relax and let the feeling of a perfect return imprint on my emotions. I'll bet she had thought I was still "sucking on" the shot that I missed. But what she didn't realize was that I hadn't felt like I had missed a shot since I restroked it with such imagery. I did not want to let anger cause me to remember the feelings and imagery of missing the shot. I was able to demonstrate to myself that I could change my attitudes and feelings about myself and lock on to a better self image of a person who is competent. I wish to reinforce the image of the type of player I'd wish to be. The psychological law which I applied is that the mind cannot distinguish between reality and what we vividly imagine.

### THE MIND CANNOT DISTINGUISH BETWEEN A REAL EXPERIENCE AND ONE THAT WE VIVIDLY IMAGINE

Maxwell Maltz

"Albert Einstein said, 'Imagination is more important than knowledge.' Knowledge of our past experiences often can cause us to have feelings of fear, while positive imagination or projection of our playing ability can lift our game to a new level. The self-talk a winner uses when he or she makes a mistake is, 'That's not like me', choosing not to identify with the mistake. I'll explain more about this later, but for the moment, John, why don't you and Steve warm up while I talk to your father."

Instead of getting
*ANGRY*
    Restroke the shot

Fig. 2

"How long has John been playing tennis, Mr. Brasky?"

"Off and on for five or six years. His grandfather played with him some and got him started. My wife's father really liked the game and played it quite religiously after he retired until his death. John has also been through a couple of tennis clinics and camps over the years."

"He looks like he has some good foundation for his strokes. Also, he doesn't seem to be lacking in enthusiasm and desire," commented Mr. Lovano as he observed the two boys playing.

"He is a hard worker, but he does better in practice than in a game. Can't seem to control his temper. I am sort of ashamed of how he acts when things don't go right."

"JOHN! Will you please play a practice set while your father and I finish talking?" Mr. Lovano yelled through the fence.

Mr. Brasky and Mr. Lovano watched as the boys began playing a set. Steve started by serving first. They hit the ball over the net a couple of times until John tried to drive a forehand down the line. The ball hit the net and he lost the point. The boys traded points back and forth. Score forty to thirty. Steve hit a soft serve which John got to easily. Taking a big swing John hit the ball out.

"DAMN, can't I do anything right?" he cried out.

"Well, there goes his temper. I hope you can do something with him," Mr. Brasky said quietly.

"Interesting," responded Mr. Lovano.

John was serving. The boys were having a nice rally until Steve hit a dinker over the net short. John ran at the ball and swung at it wildly again driving the ball into the net.

"DAMN, there's no justice!" John's composure showed signs of marked deterioration.

"Well, I think I understand the problem," Mr. Lovano said as he headed for the entrance to the courts. He walked to the net and watched them play a few more points. Steve hit a cross court backhand. John returned it deep to Steve's backhand and moved in to the net. Steve hit an easy lob. John attacked it as if to drive it into the pavement. The ball landed four feet out.

"Jeeze, there I go again!" John said under his breath.

"Stop playing for a minute. I would like to ask you a question, John," Mr. Lovano interjected.

"What's that?"

"Do you agree with this statement? If you take an idea and reinforce it with an emotion you will remember it better."

"Yeah, I guess so. Why do you ask me that?"

"Well, WHY do you want to remember your BAD shots?" asked Mr. Lovano.

"I didn't realize I was. Give me an example," John asked.

"Every time you miss a shot and get upset about it, the image of the shot you just missed is reinforced with your angry emotions. This helps to imprint the bad shot on your mind and nervous system, so the next time a similar situation occurs you have the same type of negative feelings, and therefore execute poor tennis skills. The compounding effect of all your negative emotions causes you to have a downward cycle that ends up destroying your confidence," summarized Mr. Lovano.

"Well, what am I supposed to do?" questioned John. "I want to play well and I get mad when I don't."

"What you need to do is restroke your shot with as much feeling and confidence as if you had hit it perfectly. Breathe out as if you are restroking the shot to give the body a sense of relaxation. This will take some conscious practice at first but it will become quite natural. Remember what I just told you before, **THE MIND CANNOT DISTINGUISH BETWEEN A REAL EXPERIENCE AND ONE THAT YOU VIVIDLY IMAGINE.** Replaying the stroke you missed in your mind and adding the angry emotions just has a way of destroying your confidence. Restroking the shot using appropriate movement patterns is what you need to do. Try this the next time you miss a shot. To improve we must identify with the image of how we want to act. Reacting negatively causes us to wallow in our mistakes. Learning to use your emotions in a positive manner is a powerful tool in maximizing your potential. Now, let me watch you play a few more points."

The boys continued their game. Steve hit an easy forehand drive to John. John attacked it in his usual manner and hit it long. He started to get angry.

"**RESTROKE YOUR SHOT**, John. Imagine and feel what it is like to hit a perfect forehand deep and across the court."

John regained his composure and returned to the place where he had missed the shot and swung his racket as if hitting a properly placed cross court shot. As they continued to play, John worked to stay under control. He had to remind himself whenever he missed a shot, to practice what Mr. Lovano had said. Mr. Lovano reminded and encouraged him a few times. The rallies became longer as John settled down.

At the end of the practice session Mr. Lovano gave John an audio cassette tape and made an appointment with John and his father to come to his home and take some tests on the computer.

"John, I want you to set thirty minutes aside every day next week to listen to that tape, Maximizing Your Potential. Find a place where you can be alone, like in your bedroom. Try to eliminate any outside distractions," instructed Mr. Lovano.

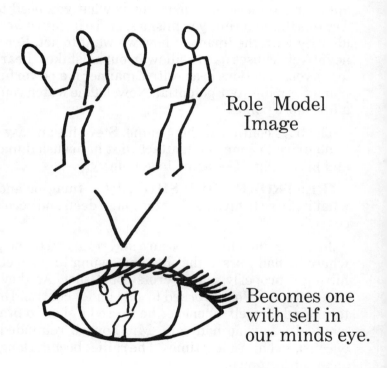

Role Model
Image

Becomes one
with self in
our minds eye.

The mind cannot distinguish between reality and what we vividly imagine.

Fig. 3

# 3

# TENNIS ON THE MIND

*To understand ourselves and others around us is the beginning and end of education.*

Krishnammurti

"I see you didn't have any trouble finding my place," Mr. Lovano said as John's father parked the car.

"Your instructions were easy to follow," replied Mr. Brasky.

"Glad to see you both here. I think you will find this morning quite interesting. I have a number of things I would like to have you try. John, do you like computers?" questioned Mr. Lovano.

"Sure, we have a computer at home and I use them at school."

They entered the house and headed for Mr. Lovano's office in the basement. The office wasn't very big and there were sailing pictures on the walls. A computer was sitting on the desk.

"I have the program loaded in the machine. You can answer the questions by using the joy stick. John, we'll let you go first. The program is called *Personality Analyzer*. You'll notice on the screen that it will display a short statement which can be answered by one of the two words below. You are to make your selection by moving the joy stick to the right or left depending on the degree to which it completes the statement. I'll be talking to your dad in the other room. Any questions, John?"

"No, this is easy."

"Pretty high tech approach you have. Personality test on computers, biofeedback, and relaxation tapes. I listened to the cassette tape you gave John and it was very interesting. Would you tell me more about why you use all of these tools?" inquired Mr. Brasky.

"Well, in the first place we live in a very fast-paced society. We all should set aside some time to relax. When we relax, our minds can still be occupied with pleasant things we like to do. The first part of the tape takes the listener through an exercise of guided relaxation. This gets the body relaxed and allows the mind to be more receptive to the information, because the mind is more receptive to auditory information when the body is relaxed. After the tape guides the listener to a relaxed state, one experiences pleasant descriptions of seeing themselves on the tennis court playing beautifully and in control. Techniques for breathing which will help a person control anxiety and tension while playing are described. This information imprints on our subconscious the type of reaction and self-talk needed in the tense moments of a match. One needs to have a positive attitude and practice positive self-talk, because in the heat of the competition fear and anxiety may cause our bodies to tense up and repeat old patterns of failure. Negative performance is accompanied by negative self-talk. Like saying to oneself 'Well stupid, you screwed up again.' The audio tape programs the mind with appropriate responses to overcome the negative responses. I believe the game of tennis is over fifty percent mental skills and the rest, physical. Learning to play tennis well is a lesson in stress management and thought control. Tension will build up inside if one has conflicting thoughts and feelings going on between the conscious and the subconscious mind. The subconscious is a very powerful force which has a greater effect on our performance than many of us wish to admit. Psychologists are making inroads into understanding how we can learn to take control of what is imprinted on the subconscious. The Eastern mystics have used techniques to program the subconscious for thousands of years. Just like a computer chip that can be programmed to follow a set of complex instructions, people can program their subconscious mind to work for them rather than against them."

"Interesting. How can I learn more about this?" questioned Mr. Brasky.

"I'll give you a list of books and tapes which explain these concepts in more detail. The book, *A Mind's Eye*, a good start. We must understand how our thoughts and belief systems determine how we react and what we become. Mankind can learn how to control its destiny. We are what we think. We can either program ourselves for success or failure. We must take control of our thoughts. These ideas have been around for centuries, but not widely accepted or understood. Here is a copy of a story I found in a book of Zen Buddhism which exemplifies the need for mental preparation in order to build self-confidence before an athletic event.

## O-Nami the Wrestler

A wrestler named O-Nami, Great Waves, was immensely strong and highly skilled in the art of wrestling. In private he defeated even his very teacher, but in public his own young pupils could throw him.

In his trouble he went to a Zen master who was stopping at a nearby temple by the sea, and asked for counsel.

"Great Waves is your name," said the master, "so stay in this temple tonight, and listen to the waves of the sea. Imagine you are those waves. Forget that you are a wrestler, and become those huge waves sweeping everything before them." And the teacher left.

O-Nami remained. He tried to think only of the waves, but he thought of many things. Then gradually he did think only of the waves. They rolled larger and larger as the night wore on. They swept away the flowers in the vases before the Buddha. They swept away the vases. Even the bronze Buddha was swept away. By dawn the temple was only surging water, and O-Nami sat there with a faint smile on his face. That day he entered the public wrestling, and won every bout. From that day, no one in Japan could ever throw him.

"I'll go check on John. He should be just about through," Mr. Lovano said and headed for his office. "Okay, we can print out the results and let your Dad take the test.

"Mr. Brasky, are you comfortable with computers?"

"Yes, we have computers at work, and also one at home that the kids let me use sometimes."

"Mr. Brasky, John and I will go in the other room while you take your turn with the computer. Holler if you need any assistance."

"Mr. Lovano, that is sort of a neat program, but what did it tell us?" questioned John.

"Well, according to how you answered the questions, your character and temperament type came out ESTP; that means you are more extroverted than introverted, more sensate than intuitive, more thinking than feeling, and more perceiving than judging. According to Dr. Kiersey in his book, *Please Understand Me*, here is a list of the strengths of people with your same temperament. Mr. Lovano showed it to John.

"The results from Dr. Kiersey's studies and tests will help us to understand you better and give us clues to your individual learning style. Our learning style is related to our temperament. People have different temperaments and may not be of the same temperament as you are. I need to understand how you learn best if I am going to be effective when I work with you, and this means my approach to coaching you should be geared to your style."

"What is temperament anyway?" asked John.

"Temperament is a word used to describe the characteristics of our behavior. How we respond to people, things, ideas, and stress. The demands of our environment," responded Mr. Lovano.

"How do we get it? Are we born with this temperament or is the behavior learned?" John asked.

"From my studies it appears to be some of both."

"What do you mean by subconscious? I'm not sure I understand that idea either," asked John with a puzzled look.

"It is the thoughts or feelings that are not part of your conscious mind, and not directly under your control. One might have the goal in mind of wanting to play well, but subconsciously have the feeling that he or she is probably going to lose."

"Is our temperament part of our conscious or our subconscious mind?" John asked.

"That's a good question! Our temperament is a manifestation of our conscious and subconscious mind. Many psychologists feel that we should get in touch with our subconscious mind, since it is where we discover our higher self and uncover our own Godliness. Our own creativity and strength flows out from within our inner being. Also, our temperament is our way of adapting to our environment, such as the way we deal with stress and anxiety. For example, the game of tennis will put you under a lot of stress at times. My understanding of your temperament can help me design mental training exercises to fit your needs. I also have another program called *Performance Inventory Analyzer* which will further identify your mental strengths and weaknesses."

"Does the subconscious have anything to do with how I play tennis?" inquired John.

"Tennis is a game of confidence. Confidence grows out of our subconscious minds and is based on deep seated feelings about ourselves. Out there on the court is life in a small drama. People who don't even know you can see that your true self is completely exposed when being driven to your limits. When I am off my game it is usually because I press too hard, have lapses in concentration, or begin to fear failure. My mind is wandering and out of control. I had to practice mental exercises to focus my mind and displace fear with desire. Learning to displace fear with desire will be one of your greatest challenges," stated Mr. Lovano.

"Then you are saying fear or desire are what motivate us?" restated John.

"Yes, they are the things which compel us to act. A fearful person sees the present through the eyes of the failures of the past, whereas a person driven by desire has a vision for the future based on hope, love, and joyous anticipation. The use of guided imagery helps to displace the thoughts and feelings of fear with hope and desire. The winner says 'I can, I want to, and the loser says, 'I can't, I have to.' The subconscious controls the quality of our effort and either frees us to attain our greatest potential or holds us back in mediocrity. We either hold onto a vision of success or live in fear. To remain neutral is to turn off the emotions and lose the spark that makes life exciting. We are all potent individuals if we get in touch with our hidden desires and find constructive outlets to fulfill them."

"My impression of how I should improve my game was to hit more tennis balls and practice harder and longer. Now you're telling me I should budget as much time for practicing my mental game off the court as I do practicing my tennis strokes on the court. I'm beginning to see what you're saying," John said, tilting his head to one side.

"Hitting two thousand tennis balls when one is in the wrong state of mind causes the mind, body, and spirit to work against each other. The wrong feelings and thoughts can become linked together. Any thoughts of fear or failure will cause the wrong outcome, because thoughts held in mind produce after their kind. Fear tenses the body, causing us to make mistakes, while positive desires unite all of our abilities to produce our greatest efforts."

"Why don't they teach us about the development of the mental side of the game when we are very young so we can begin early to get it all together?" asked John.

"I guess because it is hard to explain to young people, especially if they think they have all the answers. I was well into my thirties when I began to understand how my mental, spiritual, and physical being work together. When we are first learning the game of tennis or life, our minds seem to play tricks on us as they uncontrollably pass from the thought of fear of failure to desire to succeed. As we practice the mental game we learn how to replace fear with desire. Ultimately we wish to go beyond desire, to play in a state of mindlessness. Our whole being plays for the sheer joy of movement. Strokes seem to happen naturally. Hitting a perfect shot is all that matters, blending our energies with the racket to become one entity. The game is no longer a game, but a dance of our spirit.

"Here is an audio tape I would like to have you listen to every night before going to sleep. Let's set up another lesson for Saturday morning."

# 4

# MORNING LESSON

**Confidence is not an accident, it is the result of one's will.**

Mr. Lovano

It was a beautiful morning. The sky was bright blue and the air was still as John bicycled to the corner of Sixth and Peabody to meet Mr. Lovano. John and Mr. Lovano would be bicycling across town to the college tennis courts for the morning lesson. Pedaling standing up John raced along Main Street while his mind was preoccupied with visions of being on the tennis court hitting beautiful strokes and having infinite energy. The thoughts brought on flashes of exhilaration and joy as the feeling of a perfectly hit stroke trickled up his arm. He could feel that today was going to be a wonderful experience on the court. His anticipation was building as he looked down the block; Mr. Lovano was waiting for him at the corner, leaning against his bicycle. His bike was a light blue twelve-speed with a bag on the front for carrying tennis balls.

"Good morning, John. Well, the way you rode up it looks like you have lots of energy this morning."

"I'm feeling good and I have been playing a mental game while riding my bike. I hit some fantastic shots in my mind that really felt great. I just hope I can repeat it on the tennis court."

"Know that you can play fantastically and affirm it to yourself. Confidence is built off the court as well as on. The player you become is a result of the visions projected in your dreams and imagination. It is important to program your mind for success so that you will feel comfortable when you get there. This is done by previewing the forthcoming events using mental rehearsal. Many people neglect the power of thought and imagery when trying to build their confidence. As Dr. Maxwell Maltz said, 'All your actions, feeling, behavior, and even your abilities, are always consistent with the self-image," responded Mr. Lovano.

"What do you mean by self-image?" questioned John.

"It is the type of person we perceive ourselves to be. In any situation, whether it be on the tennis court or taking a test in school, we have a preconceived notion of what our behavior will be in that situation."

"Let's get to the courts so I can see if my mental preparation has helped my game. I listened to the relaxation tape last night just before going to sleep. When I was waking up this morning I was having vivid dreams of playing beautiful tennis. It was a neat feeling. Right now I feel very confident. I hope I don't lose this feeling."

"It might happen, but affirm to yourself that if it does you will concentrate on your breathing and know the confidence will return as long as one doesn't worry about the lack of it. Worry and fear will chase confidence away.

Confusion results when we have opposing thoughts and emotions, like wanting to do well and fearing you won't. Commit to yourself how you want to perform rather than worry about performing poorly. That is why it is best to give thanks for infinite confidence knowing it is a gift of God."

"What do you mean confidence is a gift from God?" questioned John.

"In an effort to understand the spiritual part of myself and build my confidence, I have studied information about psychology, philosophy, and religion. The truths I found have been around for centuries, but I was not aware of them. Jesus Christ was one of the greatest psychologists of all time because He had such a good understanding of man's psyche. In order to build confidence and displace fear we can use the magic of believing. Jesus said it this way, 'What things soever ye desire, when ye pray, believe that ye receive them, and ye shall have them.' Giving thanks for confidence to the supreme power in the universe takes our minds off worrying."

"Sounds crazy. To believe you have something and to give thanks for it, even if you're not sure you're going to get it or don't think you have it. I don't know if I can buy that. It kind of goes against the way we are taught about other things in school," John replied, with a skeptical look on his face.

"Well, you will get a chance to experiment with the magic of believing as you learn the inner game of tennis. Let's go. Marlene will be waiting for us and I'm looking forward to the ride up the hill to the tennis courts."

"It's a steep climb. I'm not so sure I am looking forward to it."

"We have to ride up the hill anyway, so love your adversity and challenges. Love will displace dread and fear. Also, this is a good chance to test the ideas I have been talking about," Mr. Lovano said with a twinkle in his eye.

*It was a leisurely ride the ten blocks to Liberty Street where the hill got steeper. Mr. Lovano always chose the route which was most difficult. He said it allowed him to concentrate on his breathing when he felt his body start to complain. The mind to him was much stronger than the body. One must focus on breathing and not focus on muscle tensing or 'muscle hurting.' Correct breathing helps to control anxiety. Exhale and let the tension out with each breath.*

"I sort of stumbled onto the fact that riding my bike to the tennis court cleared my mind from problems of the day and got my body ready to play tennis," Mr. Lovano said as he reached the top of the hill. "The discovery has helped me play better with less warm-up and also has provided a time of transition when I moved from one activity to another."

The courts were behind the college in a secluded setting among the trees. Marlene was sitting quietly on the bench outside the courts and didn't pay any attention to John's and Mr. Lovano's arrival. She appeared to be deep in thought. A light green racing bike was parked near her.

"Is she my practice partner? I hope she doesn't mind my hitting as hard as I can. I really feel like playing aggressively," John said boldly.

"I think you don't have to worry. Marlene may look as if she is better at modeling tennis clothes than playing tennis, but you will see that her strength is hidden inside," Mr. Lovano said as he waved to her. Marlene shyly waved back.

"I'm not afraid to play tennis with a girl. They are the weaker sex anyway," John said with an air of arrogance.

"How long have you been waiting, Marlene? I don't think we're late," Mr. Lovano said as he looked at his watch.

"No, you're not late. I just planned to arrive ten minutes early so I could compose myself and play a little mental tennis the way you have taught me," Marlene said as she winked at Mr. Lovano.

"Good, I want you to meet John. He has just started lessons with me. I am helping him prepare for a tournament that's to be held at the end of next month," Mr. Lovano stated as he removed paper and a clipboard from his bike bag. "Why don't the two of you warm up on the end court?"

John and Marlene started hitting the ball back and forth. Marlene's strokes were very smooth and she did not seem to be in a hurry or over-anxious. John, on the other hand, was aggressive and tried to hit as hard as he could.

It was inspiring to watch Marlene move to the ball. She didn't waste any motion, fluidly hitting the ball with confidence, and was always in the right place at the right time. Hitting the ball on the rise she redirected all of John's energy back to him. John hit a strong approach shot to her backhand and moved to the net. Marlene put up a short lob which John hammered into the forehand corner for a winner.

Marlene returned to the spot from which she had hit the ball. She perfectly restroked the shot with the same feeling and concentration as if this was the most important shot she had hit in her life, even though she was hitting an imaginary ball. After she had restroked the shot, she looked across the net to watch the imaginary ball land perfectly in the corner and smiled as if she had hit a perfect backhand lob. They continued to warm up for a few more minutes until Mr. Lovano interrupted.

"I would like you to play a set and I will do some charting of your game. John, remember what I said about restroking your shots."

"Oh, sure," John said half-heartedly.

Marlene smiled at Mr. Lovano as he said it. John let Marlene serve first. She took a number of warm-up serves before beginning. Her serve was not slow nor fast but it was consistently placed deep into the corners. Feeling ready to start the first game, she hit a well placed spin serve to John's backhand. Attacking it aggressively, and not taking into account the spin of the ball, John hit it into the net. He appeared to show no emotion; he just stopped and looked at where it hit the net. The next serve in the ad court was a flat serve to his forehand which John hit explosively down the line for a winner. Marlene congratulated him on the nice shot, then walked back to where she served and pretended to hit another serve in the ad court. Again she re-enacted it as if she had hit a perfect serve and then took another stroke as if she had actually gotten to his shot and returned it. The score was fifteen-all. The next point was a good rally until Marlene hit a ball short to John. Taking advantage of the opportunity, he hit deep to her backhand and advanced to a position three feet from the net. Marlene hit a beautiful lob deep to the backhand side like the one she had hit in her imagination earlier in the game. John moved back, but because he was off balance, his overhead smash struck the court two feet out.

"Damn, can't I do anything right?" John said under his breath.

Mr. Lovano didn't say anything, just penciled some marks on his chart. The next two points were long rallies as Marlene continued to hit balls that cleared the net by eight to ten feet and landed deep in the backcourt. John would be impatient and overstroke the ball, hitting one wide and an other into the net. He would grit his teeth and clench his fist as he watched them go out. It was forty-fifteen as Marlene served a slow spinning ball wide to John's forehand. John went for the kill and hit it long.

"Is there no justice?" he said as he dropped his racket. **"GOD HELP ME!"**

Mr. Lovano couldn't stand it any more and stepped onto the court, shaking his head with a half smile on his face.

"John, I see you have forgotten something we had talked about before."

"What's that?" he said almost defiantly.

"Using your imagination to redirect your thinking; restroking your shots," reminded Mr. Lovano.

"Well, I feel kind of foolish doing it and I'm not sure it is necessary."

"Speaking about feeling or looking foolish, you look more foolish losing your temper and letting your game fall apart. Each time you miss a shot and get frustrated with yourself you start building up tension in your body. This negative energy is really destructive to your playing ability and confidence. How do you feel now?" asked Mr. Lovano.

"Not very good! I would like to tear the cover off a tennis ball. I feel all tense inside."

"I imagine you do. You probably have all sorts of negative feelings. Emotional stresses such as anger, worry, anxiety, and self-doubt are written all over your face. Right now your brain is robbed of proper nutrients by the constricted blood flow caused by these emotions. Your mind tends to focus on the last error or loss, rather than focusing on the at hand. Negative emotions of this kind have a hypnotic influence. The physical effects are felt almost instantly. Mental concentration can be vastly diminished, accompanied by weakening of volition - the determination to win. Another way of putting it is **YOU'RE CHOKING!**" lectured Mr. Lovano. "Marlene, do you mind practicing your serve while I have some time alone with John?"

"Okay! Do you have some tennis cans I can use for targets?" asked Marlene.

"Sure, they are in the bike bag."

Mr. Lovano and John walked away from the court toward a large shade tree where they sat on the freshly mowed grass.

"John, I would like to share some information about myself and how I learned some of these principles of how the mind, body, and spirit work together. During the winter months prior to the start of tennis season my thoughts would be joyfully filled with anticipation of getting out on the court and playing magnificent tennis. I would vividly imagine myself hitting the strokes perfectly. When I got out on the court the first time I was amazed at how well I played. I would stroke my forehand with confidence. As the season progressed I would begin to lose my confidence and hit my forehand tentatively. I would start the season with confidence and then the confidence would disappear. This puzzled me, because it happened many years in succession. I tried to understand why this was happening. At the first of the season I was confident, but then the fear and anxiety would creep in and the strokes would fall apart.

"It wasn't until I realized how our mind stores images and feelings that I realized how I was unconsciously destroying my own confidence. Our minds are like video cameras which take pictures of the things we do or that happen to us. The interesting thing is that the mind also records along with the picture the emotional feelings we have at the time the incident occurs.

"Going back to the problem of losing confidence in my forehand, I would start out the season with a positive attitude, playing strongly and smoothly...then my game would start falling apart. What happened was that I would miss a shot which was normally easy for me; then I would get upset about missing the shot and replay the point in my mind as a negative event. I didn't realize that dwelling on the missed shot reinforced in my mind a self-image that I was a person who misses easy forehand shots. Remember that the mind can record images and the body will hold onto the emotional feelings linked to that image."

John looked puzzled then said, "I can see myself doing the same thing, but when we do something wrong shouldn't we spend time thinking about it?"

"Sure, a person should learn from his mistakes. My mistake was not missing the shot but getting upset about it and holding onto the negative self-image. There are certain psychological laws which govern how our minds and bodies work together. The one that applies is: If you take an idea or image in the mind and reinforce it with an you will remember it better."

**IF YOU TAKE AN IDEA OR IMAGE
IN THE MIND AND REINFORCE
IT WITH AN EMOTION YOU
WILL REMEMBER IT BETTER**

I like to watch other people play tennis. The important thing to watch sometime is not all the great shots, but the errors they make and how they deal with the mistake. Let's look at what was happening while playing with Marlene. The first few times you missed a shot, you only showed a small amount of emotion, but when you made a number of errors in succession, the frustration began to build. The thoughts and feelings of each missed shot add to those of the previous one and your confidence begins to evaporate. Vic Braden, a psychologist and tennis coach who has done a lot of studies of the game of tennis, observed that beginning tennis players make many more errors than good shots. In fact errors outnumber unforced errors 30 to 1. In intermediate tennis errors outnumber unforced errors 20 to 1 and even in pro tennis the ratio is 10 to 1. Therefore, when we play tennis we will make more errors than great shots. Even if you win you will make more errors than great shots. That is why it is important to know how to deal with all this negativity because it can be shattering to a person's self-image. Why do you get mad on the tennis court?" asked Mr. Lovano.

"Because I know I can play better than I am playing. I want to do well."

"That's understandable. If two players are equal in stroking ability, the person who will win is the one who is able to handle his or her emotion constructively. The player who gets all upset is destroying his own confidence. Do you agree with the statement, **IF YOU TAKE AN IDEA AND REINFORCE IT WITH AN EMOTION YOU WILL REMEMBER IT BETTER?**"

"Yeah, you told me that once before," replied John.

"Hearing a truth does not mean we will necessarily apply it. It is only when experience demonstrates its validity that we have the 'ah-so' experience of enlightenment.

Every time you miss a shot and get upset about it, I wonder what you expect to accomplish. Getting upset is using your emotions. Therefore, you have the idea or picture in your mind of missing a shot and you reinforce the idea by getting upset. **WHY IS IT THAT YOU WANT TO REMEMBER THAT YOU ARE A PERSON WHO MISSES EASY SHOTS?"**

"Oh, I didn't realize it worked that way. What should I do?"

"Restroke your shot and hit it in your mind's eye perfectly, as you had really intended to do it. Try to see it going just where you wanted it to go and exhale as you stroke to give yourself a feeling of relaxation and confidence. This will imprint in your mind a perfectly hit shot. Next time the situation comes up your chances of hitting properly will be greatly enhanced. Remember the other psychological law of the mind that comes into action.

## THE MIND CANNOT DISTINGUISH BETWEEN A REAL EXPERIENCE AND ONE THAT IS VIVIDLY IMAGINED

"Did you notice what Marlene did when she mis-hit a ball or was caught out of position? She went back and replayed the shot."

"I am beginning to understand now that you point it out to me," John replied.

"Let's try a little experiment. Close your eyes and visualize green. See in your mind's eye a green piece of paper or a green lawn. Okay, can you see something green?" Mr. Lovano waited a few minutes so John could center in on the image in his mind.

"I can see something green. It's not hard to do."

"Next, let's try to change the state of our emotions. Try to feel angry. See if you can let the emotion take over your consciousness," Mr. Lovano said.

A minute or so elapsed before John said anything. "I really don't feel like doing that and I am having difficulty doing it."

"Okay, let's try this. Put your hands over your head. Hold them straight up in the air. Good, I see you didn't have any trouble doing that."

"What's this all supposed to show me?"

"Well, you can see the easiest thing to do is to put your hands over your head. The second easiest is to see an image in your mind. The hardest thing to do sometimes is change your state of emotions. So when you start missing shots and restroke them and try to visualize a perfectly hit shot, it distracts you from letting any frustration or anger build up. As William Glasser says in his book, *Take Effective Control Of Your Life*, we don't get angry. Instead we start **ANGERING**. That is, we let one incident build on another until we have become upset and lose our composure. Therefore, we don't get frustrated, we start **FRUSTRAT-ING**. It is a process we let happen to ourselves by not using an act of will to divert our attention to that which we wanted to happen."

"Thinking back to what I was doing while playing, I can see myself **ANGERING**. Can we go back on the tennis court and try again? I felt so sure of myself while riding up here on my bike. I wondered where that feeling went," John said, warming to the idea.

Fig. 4

"Before going back on the court let's take a few minutes and practice some guided imagery to help you center yourself. Close your eyes and focus in on your breathing. Sit comfortably with the spine straight, but not rigid. Know that the world outside of you is at peace when the world inside of you is at peace. Tension and anxiety are created when you are out of touch with the inner voice that guides us. Inner peace is a gift of spirit when we let go of fear thoughts and choose to be still. Think back to the moments of awakening this morning, when your mind was bringing forward thoughts and feelings of being out on the tennis court and playing beautifully. As you breathe out, let any frustration flow out, and as you breathe in, let the vision of the tennis player you wish to be appear on the video screen of your mind. See yourself confident and in 'relaxed control', able to float up to the ball. Stroke with fluidness, knowing that all you have to do is project your thought and the ball will go there. Know that if the ball goes out or into the net you will not hold onto that image, but rather let it go. Return to the spot where it was hit and replay the shot, returning it perfectly.

"John, repeat these statements after me to yourself. I remember that no one can control my thoughts if I do not focus on my emotions. I will use my energy and emotions constructively. I know that my game will be lifted to a new level as long as I am attuned with the moment. Playing tennis is my chance to act out my part in a human drama. My confidence will always be with me as long as I return to that place of inner peace. In a few moments you can open your eyes, but only when you are ready."

"Whew, that felt good? I had such a good feeling and it still lingers with me. Can we go back on the tennis court? I have something I need to do there," John stated as he arose and stretched like a cat.

## Centering the Absence of Fear

Fig. 5

"Yes, that's fine. Why don't you practice some serves and service returns with Marlene?"

John entered the court and got into position to return Marlene's serve. The ball hit the backhand corner in the deuce court. John swung smoothly and met the ball solidly. The ball cleared the net by two feet and landed one foot from the baseline. Marlene was caught off guard and the ball landed at her feet, skidded by, and hit the fence. After a moment she returned to the baseline and returned an imaginary ball to John. John smiled and yelled to Marlene, **"NICE RETURN!"**, then looked over to Mr. Lovano who was smiling.

# 5

# VOLITION

**Success is not an accident. People cannot expect to be accidentally good.**

Mr. Lovano

That afternoon Mr. Lovano invited John over to his house to investigate different approaches to uncovering the roadblocks that inhibit success. He said the tools he used were designed to allow an individual to get in touch with attitudes or feelings that are below the conscious level of thought. It sounded kind of scary to John, but Mr. Lovano was such a reassuring and positive person, that it seemed okay to try other approaches.

The bicycle ride to his house was two miles from school and allowed John time to think about his aspirations in tennis. Pedaling steadily, but not in a hurry, he took a route through the back streets. Thoughts about Marlene drifted into his mind as he visualized the calm, self-assured way she played tennis.

*I wonder if she was always that way ... before she started taking lessons from Mr. Lovano. I can't imagine Marlene not being a picture of grace and confidence on the tennis court. I hope we'll see more of each other.*

Marlene invited John over Friday night to view some video tapes of tennis. John's mind continued to play with thoughts of the upcoming date as he rounded the corner.

John rode his bike up the driveway and parked it inside the garage. An uneasy feeling overtook him as he thought about what he was doing there. Hesitantly, his finger pushed the door bell. A few moments later Mr. Lovano appeared.

"Hi, John, you're right on time. I hope you are ready to enter the space age as we explore some of the equipment I have. Does it bother you to be trying any of these things?"

"Oh, I guess not," he replied sheepishly.

"The first thing I am going to do is hook you up to the biofeedback equipment and let you get in touch with different states of relaxation. What I have found out about myself is that getting in tune to the feeling of relaxation can help me see the world differently. Under stress we store tension in the muscles of our eyebrows and forehead, as well as other parts of our body. The sensor will be attached to your forehead to give you feedback on subtle changes in the muscle tension. What we wish to accomplish is how to control your relaxation response. Relax your forehead will require you to get the feeling of looking at things with 'soft eyes'. Relaxing the eyebrows and area around the bridge of the nose. Looking with 'soft eyes' is an expression used by Eastern culture. The technique will evoke a different consciousness and awareness and can be used to calm ourselves. Relaxation is a key to reaching our ideal performance state. Here, sit down at the computer, and I will put this headband on your forehead. The headband is hooked to a device called an electromyograph or EMG. The electromyograph measures the amount of electrical discharge in the skeletal muscle fibers. The discharge is translated into a visual display on the computer monitor, which you can observe as changes in the graph. Use this feedback to get in touch with minute changes in your muscle tension. The changes in the graph on the screen are directly proportional to the amount you contract or relax the muscles in your forehead.

"What do my thoughts and muscle tension in my forehead have to do with each other?" asked John.

"Edmund Jacobsen, one of the early pioneers of EMG training, found that every thought and emotional state had a corresponding muscle activity. The activity is small and not usually a part of our conscious awareness. The EMG amplifies small changes in muscle tension and allows you to become aware of the relationship between your thoughts, feelings, and the corresponding muscle activities. Jacobsen found that anxious patients showed elevated levels of muscle tension. Playing good tennis requires us to manage stress. Have you ever felt tension building inside of you when you're playing an important point?" questioned Mr. Lovano.

"Yes, but I have never known what to do when I felt that way," John said uncomfortably.

"Well, let's experiment. We'll get the machine adjusted and I'll turn on a tape for you to listen to and you can practice relaxing."

Mr. Lovano turned on a tape recorder. The tape explained how the biofeedback machine worked and gave John instructions on how to move different parts of his body, and observe the results on the screen. The line on the graph began dropping to lower levels as John let go and began relaxing.

The tape told John:

As you consciously feel the minute difference in muscle tension, tell yourself that it is okay to relax. Know that you can do it. As you let go of any negative thoughts, feel a calmness come over you. Imagine yourself out on the tennis court. It is a beautiful day. Your strokes are strong and consistent. All you have to do is project your thoughts and the ball will be hit there automatically. You are full of energy and playing in control. If any feeling of stress or anxiety comes to your consciousness, relax the forehead and brow as you are doing now. As you relax, your fears will melt away. To be present in the moment is all you are asked. You are totally focused on the present. Concentration is so easy that actions are anticipated before they occur. A sense of extraordinary power seems to appear ... possibly from an outside source or from a new source within oneself. You are completely immersed in the activity, perfectly in tune with the action on the court. A feeling of joy and ecstasy comes over you."

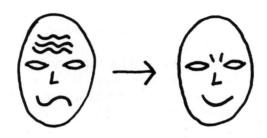

## "Soft Eyes"

Concentrate on relaxing your brow. As you begin to relax, your fears will melt away. You will be perfectly in time with the action on the court.

Fig. 6

Ten or fifteen minutes elapsed before Mr. Lovano returned. John was very quiet and did not move as Mr. Lovano entered the room.

"How are you doing, John? May I interrupt you?" he asked softly.

"Okay... that was interesting. A real different feeling. A whole tennis match flashed through my mind. I played my best game ever. Tell me more about what is going on," John inquired with calm intensity.

"What I am trying to do is reach you on your deepest level, to get beyond the ego or intellect to the creative subconscious. Many people deny that the subconscious even exists and therefore do not even try to work with it, but what I hope to show you is that if you can harness the power of the subconscious, you will find it is the most powerful force given to man. Learn how to use your subconscious power constructively and it will move your game to new levels. Let it go unchecked and it can bring forth inappropriate feelings and responses that can be detrimental to your performance. The key to accessing it is imagining and visualizing in a relaxed state," explained Mr. Lovano.

"Do other athletes use these kinds of techniques?"

"Yes, the importance of mental preparation is becoming more widely accepted and practiced. Abraham Maslow saw that there were people in all walks of life who know, either intuitively or through rigorous discipline, how to harness the hidden powers of their mind and thus to approach, equal, or improve upon their peak performances time and time again. Maslow referred to them as 'self-actualizing' people, who assumed control of the mental and physical skills to perform optimally on a fairly consistent basis."

"Which tennis players practice these techniques?" John asked.

"Many, I'm sure. A couple of years ago, I saw Ken Rosewall play tennis in the Masters Tournament in Seattle. Rosewall was one of the great tennis players to come out of Australia who played on the pro circuit in the fifties and sixties. When I saw him he was fifty years old and still playing beautiful tennis, in fact leading the Masters standing. What was interesting to watch was his presence on the court. At first glance he looked hypnotized or half awake. He seemed to play in a relaxed state of consciousness. His strokes were fluid and graceful. Nothing seemed to bother him or spoil his state of consciousness. I think he is one of those 'self-actualizing' athletes Maslow was talking about. Studies have shown that high level athletes can make their brain waves change to alpha state. This altered state of consciousness allows them to be more aware of what is going on in a match and to react faster. Their anticipation and awareness is at a high level, almost as if they can read their opponent's mind."

"What should I do on the tennis court to make this work for me?" John asked with anticipation.

"You have thirty seconds between points. Take this time to focus your attention while thinking and feeling as if the biofeedback headband were on your forehead and you were concentrating on relaxing your brow and looking with 'soft eyes'. With a little practice it will come to you very easily," reassured Mr. Lovano.

"I always thought concentration was something we had to work very hard at while doing it."

"You don't have to try harder, but rather try softer. Relaxed concentration is letting go. It's like floating in air. You're there but you're not. All of your receptors are activated, but not necessarily focused," Mr. Lovano explained. "I will give you another chance to try it again some other time.

"Now, I would like to play with something called 'mind mapping'. In Gabrielle Lusser Rico's book, *Writing The Natural Way*, she calls this technique a 'nonlinear brainstorming process akin to free association.' The process is used to access thoughts and feelings just below the conscious level of thinking. The writing exercise can lead us to parts of our mind where the experiences of a lifetime mill and mingle. Here is an example I did.

"Now I want you to close your eyes and imagine the headband is on. Visualize the line on the graph dropping as you feel calm and relaxed. It is a warm spring day and you are riding up to your favorite tennis courts. See yourself entering the courts. After stretching your muscles for a few minutes you begin rallying back and forth with your partner." Mr. Lovano turned on some soft background music. "As you get in touch with your feelings and thoughts slowly open your eyes. There is a piece of white paper before you. Write the word TENNIS in the middle and circle it. Then all around it cluster thoughts or phrases which feel like they fit together. Things do not have to make sense. Let your mind play with various things you bring into the picture. Just write down whatever comes to mind."

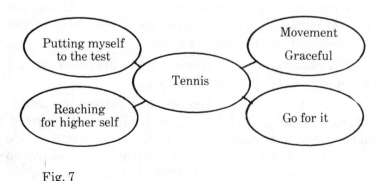

Fig. 7

While John worked, Mr. Lovano quietly left the room. The house was still except for the soft sound of piano music coming from the tape player. Five or ten minutes passed before he returned.

"Well, it looks like you explored a lot of ideas," he said as he sat down next to John. "Let's see if we can make any sense out of your mind mapping."

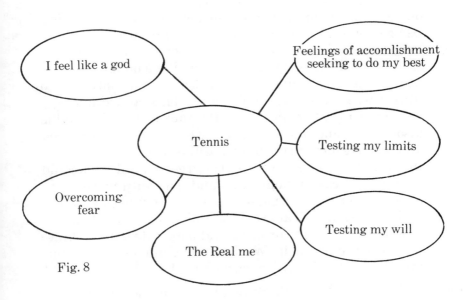

Fig. 8

"I am not surprised by what I have written. When I am playing tennis I often have many thoughts running through my head."

"Some of your comments show that you have a need to act out an inner struggle. Phrases like 'testing my will' and 'overcoming fear'. Here is an interesting one, 'I feel like a god'," stated Mr. Lovano.

"I have felt so great when I have sensed those type of peak experiences. Mr. Lovano, do you think it is wrong to state it that way? To feel godlike. That brings to mind another question. Can God help me be a better tennis player?" John asked.

"That depends! That depends on what you believe God is.

"There are many conflicting ideas on what God is and isn't. Our individual beliefs determine the impact that God has on our lives. If we see God as a person or force outside of ourself for whom we must wait for approval or blessing before we feel like one of the chosen ones, we may wait a long time before we feel we are worthy of exceptional skills or abilities. On the other hand if we believe that we are an extension or expression of God, then we only need to utilize what has been given to us. This conviction may cause a person to believe that the racket in their hand is also in the hand of God. Also, if we believe God is a good and positive force in the universe, then every movement of the racket represents different degrees of good. This could enable us to cast out our fears and play with more confidence. Otherwise, if a person doubts one's superior ability, their game may fall apart. Thoughts of fear and self doubt, if allowed to root in our mind and dominate our thinking, will break our spirit. We lose our fluidness, tense our muscles, and feel out of touch with the beauty of the game."

"But what do you think God is?" John questioned.

"I guess I have to start by explaining what I think God isn't. I chose not to believe in a concept of God as one who is watching over me like an untrusting parent just waiting for me to make a mistake so He can issue some punishment. I think we have a choice as to how we believe and what we want to believe. We will either be rewarded or punished by our beliefs. I am of the opinion that God is an omnipotent and omnipresent force in the universe. All that is good comes from God. All that is bad comes from ignorance. We must strive for pureness of heart and pureness of effort and then we will be expressing our Godliness, since we can choose to be an extension of God. I don't think He meant for us to be mediocre. The game of tennis is a microcosm of life, a small drama where we can act our our part. It gives us an opportunity to see if we can play our part with a spirit of belief about our abilities, knowing that our faith will be tested. In life it isn't who we are that makes a difference, but it is who we think we are. The person on the other side of the net isn't our adversary, but rather a mirror image of our beliefs about ourselves. When we get off our game, it isn't because the other person has gained control of us, but rather because we think he has got the upper hand," explained Mr. Lovano.

### THE POWER OF YOUR BELIEF IS THE GOVERNING FORCE IN YOUR LIFE.
Mr. Lovano

"What do you mean when you say that God is omnipresent?" asked John.

"God is always with us. It is only our fearful thoughts which keep us from seeing the presence of God or Spirit."

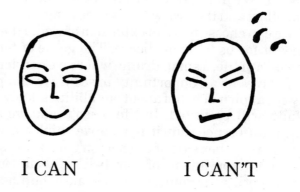

I CAN          I CAN'T

"The power of Belief
is the Governing Force
in Your Life"

Fig. 10

# 6

# MOVIES ON THE MIND

**"'Whatsoever a man soweth, that shall he also reap.' So is the way of thought. All things begin in thought. Our life unfolds as a consequence of the vision we hold in our mind's eye."**

Charles Fillmore

It was Friday, and John had been asked by Marlene to come over to her house at 7:30 P.M. It was the night they were going to watch tennis videos. Her house was located on the other side of town, a five mile trip. The bike ride would be easy since the route was basically flat and it would stay light until 9:30. A gentle, warm breeze still lingered in the air. His digital watch showed 6:50 P.M. as he swung his leg over his bike and headed down the street. Feelings of anticipation came to him as he put his weight into the pedals. Marlene was a puzzle to him.

*How could she maintain so much control and confidence on the court? What did videos about tennis have to do with building one's confidence? Mr. Lovano kept using the word volition as being a driving force in our resolve to peak performance which calls up other reserves of energy. He said our volition was fueled by many things – from past experiences of successes to recollections of live sporting events, books, and movies.*

The ride seemed to go by very quickly as John's mind wandered to thoughts of Marlene and then back to things Mr. Lovano had said. The tennis tournament was only a month away. An odd sensation came to him as he thought about putting himself to the test.

*Can I really play in control during a match as I have been doing in practice? "Be careful what you think, John," interrupted an inner voice. Oh, I must remember to change my thoughts even if that isn't how I feel at the moment ... I love to play to my limit. I love to play in control, he affirmed to himself. I guess I should focus on the card Mr. Lovano gave me.*

**WHATEVER YOU VIVIDLY IMAGINE, ARDENTLY DESIRE, SINCERELY BELIEVE, AND ENTHUSIASTICALLY ACT UPON ...MUST INEVITABLY COME TO PASS.**

Paul J. Myer

*I will hold fast to the image of the tennis player I desire to be...I will enthusiastically act upon it. My belief is building every day. God never meant for me to be mediocre. Thank you, God, for all the talent you have given me.*

## THE GARDEN OF MY MIND

**THE GARDEN OF MY MIND**
I have a Choice
What I sow I shall also reap.

Fig. 11

*Marlene's house is only two blocks away. I need to remember to ask her if she wants to play tennis in the morning. This is Elm Street and her house number is 1931. It must be on the other side of the street, near the end of the block.*

Riding up the driveway he found a place to park his bike and lock it. Trying to act very confident, he pressed the door bell.

"Hi, John. Glad you could make it," Marlene said upon opening the door.

Marlene was dressed in white slacks and a white blouse with a loosely fitting red sweater. The red and white went well with her dark hair. She led him into the living room to meet her parents. After a short introduction, they headed for the recreation room.

"How long have you been playing tennis? All your life?" he asked.

"I've been playing about four years all together, but only this last year have I felt like I understood what the game is all about. That was when I started taking lessons from Mr. Lovano. He has really helped me by showing me how I can build my confidence," Marlene responded. "Would you like to see the video about Bjorn Borg? It really has good background music."

"Why is Mr. Lovano so sold on watching videos about tennis? Does he own stock in some video company?"

"Well, Mr. Lovano said that the way to learn to play tennis is the same as how we learned to walk. Therefore, he told me to observe young children who are just learning to walk. So that is what I did. And you know what a child does first is to do a lot of observing. They program their biocomputer, the brain, with visual images. They don't need language or words when learning to walk, because a child can learn to walk before he learns to talk. The mind works with images better than language. Next, the baby will start flexing his muscles while exhibiting that 'I can' attitude in his expression. Children usually aren't afraid of failure when they are young. That is something society conditions into them. Fear of failure inhibits the natural co-ordination of the body's muscles."

"Then how can we bring this approach to learning to play tennis?" questioned John.

"Here is something Mr. Lovano gave me about mental programming."

**Jack Kramer, one of the great American tennis players commented on his forehand stroke saying, "Elsworth Vines had a classic forehand...and every forehand I ever hit after meeting him was hit with an image of how he did it."**

"Well, Mr. Lovano must intend for us to find someone to pattern our game after. That must be why he asked me who my favorite tennis player is."

"Right! Ever since we were young children we have been imitating people around us. One of the videos we can watch, is one Mr. Lovano made for me. It has pictures of Chris Evert and myself playing tennis. I am trying to pattern many of my strokes after her. Mr. Lovano said we become what we wish to be if we take direct control of what is imprinted on our mind. He told me to decide what I wanted to be and then find ways to reinforce that image on the movie screen in my mind."

"Let's watch the one about Borg first," suggested John enthusiastically.

The video began with Borg explaining the mechanics of the forehand stroke and the thoughts and feelings he has while executing it. Next, Borg is hitting the shots in slow motion with music in the background, and finally, there are pictures of Borg hitting at full speed to some very inspiring music. One is able to feel he is in Borg's shoes out on the tennis court, hitting shots just like he does with power and grace.

"That was great! It really gives you a feeling of how Borg likes to play. I liked his approach to hitting the volley, but the two-handed backhand is just not for me. My upper body doesn't seem to have the necessary flexibility, and I feel like I can hit the ball well enough using one hand. What is the video all about of you and Chris Evert Lloyd?" inquired John.

"I told Mr. Lovano that Chris was one of my favorite players and that I wanted to have a two handed backhand just like hers. We will watch it now and you will see how that video is presented."

Marlene loaded the VCR and returned to sit by John. As the video began, Chris explained her approach to the backhand stroke, how she set up for the shot, and placement of her feet. This video quickly moved into pictures of her hitting her strokes beautifully, and as if it were the most natural thing to do. Pictures of Chris were mixed with pictures of Marlene making the stroke in an identical way. As the action increased to full speed, so did the music. The music and visual effects gave feelings of movement and joy. All through the video tape pictures of Marlene hitting beautiful strokes were blended with perfect examples by Chris. The feeling was that they were one and the same person.

"Wow, it looks like every stroke you make is done with the image of how Chris does it. Have you always played that magnificently?" John asked admiringly.

"No, but watching the video gives me the feeling that I can. Mr. Lovano is pretty smart. He recorded many hours of me playing tennis. He edited out all of my bad strokes and poorly hit shots. What you are seeing here are the best strokes that I have executed and only a small percentage of the film footage. He told me to watch it four or five times a week just before going to sleep or before playing tennis.

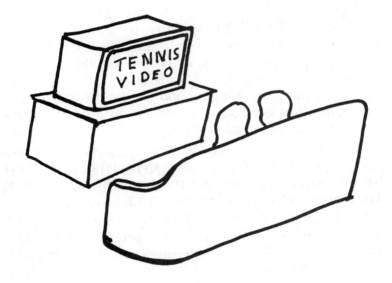

The mind works with images better
than it does with verbal explanations.

Fig. 12

Now that I think back, my game made some drastic improvement during that period. My confidence became much stronger, and I felt more natural on the court. My playing had a very different feeling to it. Sometimes I felt as if I were Chris. I didn't realize how easy it is to use my imagination as a tool to improve the self-image. I would spend a few moments every day with my eyes closed seeing Chris stroking the ball and then visualizing myself making the same stroke, moving the pictures back and forth in my mind's eye until they merged into one image. What began to happen was that I started to feel like I could stroke just like her. The thoughts of Chris hitting the ball would evoke feelings while I was playing and in turn my confidence would be increased. It just felt so natural. My game improved immensely almost overnight."

"That all makes sense because Mr. Lovano keeps reminding me that **THE MIND CANNOT DISTINGUISH BETWEEN A REAL EXPERIENCE AND ONE THAT IS VIVIDLY IMAGINED,**" John replied. "What we imagine becomes our reality. If we want to become better at something, then we have to imagine that we are. The process has a way of bringing our spirit or creative subconscious into action."

"That's right. I feel much more comfortable now, and play at a higher level. Mr. Lovano said that our self-image governs what we become. If we don't practice mentally playing at the higher level of performance then we will feel out of our comfort zone if some day we are playing very well. This uneasiness will interrupt our train of thought, causing us to make mistakes until we have lowered our performance to the level where we think we should be. Funny thing, this mental game. Make believe. Fake it until you make it. Kind of hard to admit this is what we have to do."

"Does it ever bother you that Mr. Lovano is messing around with your mind so much?" John asked.

"Not really, because he doesn't do it subversively. We talk about it and he explains how the mind, body, and spirit work together. I want to be a better tennis player and person, and I am glad to learn about some of the tools for spiritual awakening that will help me build confidence."

"The background music from the tape really sticks with me. It's just a very simple chant. JOY, JOY, JOY, JOY, EVERY NEW JOY, JOY. JOY, JOY, JOY, JOY, EVERY NEW JOY, JOY. It was sung over and over while showing pictures of you playing tenis. JOY, JOY, JOY, JOY, EVER NEW JOY. That's really powerful. Do those feelings ever come to you on the court?" John asked.

"Yes I start saying joy to myself, and that feeling starts to flow within me. It makes me feel great, as if I could keep playing forever. I feel like I have infinite energy. The group that sings it is called the Joy Singers and, boy, do you feel their inspiration. I bought a recording of theirs and every time I listen to it, if I close my eyes, I see very vivid images of playing tennis. My whole body quivers and I feel like I want to be holding onto and swinging a tennis racket. JOY, JOY, JOY, JOY, EVER NEW JOY, JOY. There goes another terrific backhand. JOY, JOY, JOY, JOY, EVER NEW JOY, JOY. I just hit a terrific forehand approach shot and volley. It is such a fun way to improve one's game. Mr. Lovano said JOY is one of the gifts of spirit, but sometimes we forget that we need to turn on the tape in our head. Some people seem to play a tape that chants DREAD, DREAD, DREAD, DREAD, EVER NEW DREAD, DREAD. Then they wonder why their energy is diminished and everything is so hard for them," Marlene said.

"I can't wait until he makes a video of me! It's eleven fifteen and I need to be going soon. Is our tennis date still on for tomorrow morning? Mr. Lovano said he might stop by to watch us play."

Marlene replied, "Maybe he'll bring his video camera."

Decide what you want to accomplish then reinforce that on the movie screen in your mind.

# 7

# TENNIS DATE

WHATEVER you can conceive in your mind and believe in your heart can be accomplished in your world.

Mr. Lovano

The sun was just breaking over the hill as John wheeled his bicycle out of the garage. This was the morning he had a date with Marlene to play tennis. Thoughts of her drifted through his mind and a feeling of excitement began to occupy his body.

*She was so beautifully feminine and yet a creature of power and grace on the tennis court. Should I hold back on my strokes and not make her look bad? I have never played a match against a girl. I don't want to do anything to injure this relationship with Marlene...but how should I act? I don't want to hold back on my game since it causes me to lose my rhythm and fluidness. What would Mr. Lovano tell me to do in this situation? Go inward. Go inward. Visualize.*

John sat down on the rock wall next to the driveway. As he made himself comfortable and still the outside world began to melt away and other images began to form in his mind.

*Images of riding to the tennis court with Marlene. Taking a few moments of quiet thought and meditation before entering the court. The time of transition. A time for meditation and prayer.*

*My performance in sports is very dependent on my mood and attention. I give thanks for all that I am to receive. Spirit is with me. I must listen to Its message. I wish to align myself with the power of good in the universe. I must remember what Mr. Lovano said about the game of tennis being a microcosm of life. It is a living example of how we interact with ourselves and other people. Our purpose in life is not to defeat other people or cause them to fail, but rather to use our energies creatively. To move through life in grace and honor. When the ball is in your court it is an opportunity to express your creativity and not plot against your opponent. Trying to mentally manipulate your opponent while trying to stroke the ball will just cause you to divide your concentration and take you further from God. To be one with the spirit is to focus all your mind on the spin of the ball and let your body flow through the stroke. To feel like you're in a twilight zone. Everything seems to slow down. I am thankful for another opportunity to hit the ball. I think this is what I am to do when I am playing with Marlene or anyone else.*

Feeling his eyes open, it seemed like hours had passed, but he had only been sitting quietly for bikes up ew to the tennis court together. It was 8:15, so there was enough was to meet Marlene at 8:30 near the fire time to tion so they could ride their ride leisurely to where they were to meet.

It felt good to be riding along. The warm early morning air brushed by. Not too hot or cold. Just fresh and clean. The street started to climb as John moved the shift lever back to a lower gear. A little more adjustment was needed as he tuned out the rattle in the chain. Sometimes it felt as if he and the bike were one entity, a blend of energy, muscles, and balance with lightweight alloys. A perfect complement. Extending his hand, he nudged the lever forward and the wheels began to spin faster. A rush of energy flowed through his body. Another nudge of the shift lever, a higher gear. The only important time in life seemed to be now, standing up on the pedals, letting his weight dig into the toe pieces, propelling the bike faster. Houses flew by out of the corner of his eye, a right turn at the corner and then two more blocks to the fire station. There it was, down at the end of the block, over on the left. He couldn't see Marlene. A glance at his watch revealed that it was 8:25.

*I made better time than I needed. What is the hurry? I hope she doesn't forget or stand me up.*

The thought of having time with her and not having to share her with others seemed almost selfish. The thought caused a different feeling to pass through his mind. Getting off his bike, he started fiddling with the cables and screws, making a minor adjustment to the brakes, testing them to make sure they would respond to a small movement of his hands. He knew how he liked the brake lever to respond to a small rotation of his wrist. As he looked up from what he was doing, he saw Marlene rounding the corner. She waved as he looked up and he waved back trying to hide the rush of excitement building inside.

"Been waiting long?" she asked as she rode up.

"Maybe ten minutes, but I spent my time adjusting my bike." John responded coolly.

"Great morning for tennis, isn't it?"

"Yes, I'm looking forward to it. Hope I can keep my mind on the ball," he said smiling at Marlene. Swinging his right leg over the bike, he kicked the stand up with his left foot. The ride to the courts was only a mile from the fire station. "Marlene, when is the last time you saw Mr. Lovano? I was hoping you might have some wisdom from him for my meditation."

"Let me see," Marlene said as she tilted her head. "The main idea he talked to me about is how fantasy is the seed of the flower of our destiny. The thoughts and images we play with in our mind grow into the realities of our life. He said that 'WHATEVER THE MIND CAN CONCEIVE, WE CAN ACHIEVE'. What we become grows out of our subconscious if we nurture it with affirmations and faith."

"Just what did Mr. Lovano mean by faith?" asked John. "Maybe the ability to hold onto feelings or thoughts knowing that with persistent effort we can become great tennis players. Why can't we be everything we want to be TODAY? Then we wouldn't have to worry whether we would attain it in the future. But then what would we have to look forward to if we were everything we wanted to be, TODAY?"

John was having to shift down since the street started to get steeper. The hardest part of the hill was the next four blocks, then the pavement leveled out.

# CONCEIVE    BELIEVE

Whatever you can conceive of
in your mind, and believe in your heart,
can be accomplished.

Fig. 13

*Life seems like an endless road of hills and plateaus. First you go up, then things level out for awhile, then you go down. It seems even kind of humorous. Up, level out, and then down, only to start over again. Mr. Lovano said that the quality of the process is more important than the goal. I've got to shift this bike into my "granny" gear to climb the next part. Forget it, John. See if you can ride up in a higher gear this time. Remember what Mr. Lovano said about raising your self-image thermostat. Increasing the challenge a little beyond past accomplishments. Look at Marlene. She seems to ride so effortlessly. She has this look of relaxed control in everything. She never seems to lose control or fight with herself. Never seems in conflict with herself. This hill feels steeper today. Oh yes, I'm in a higher gear. BREATHE, EXHALE. Let out the tension, breathe in the energy. Let your weight push down into the toe pieces. EXHALE. It's getting easier. Another block and it levels out again. I love hills, especially when I am nearing the top and know I can catch my breath. Take it easy for awhile.*

"Marlene, do you like riding up hills?" John gasped.

"What hills? Did we ride up a hill?" she answered with a smile and a teasing glint in her eye.

As they rounded the corner the courts came into view. Two players were practicing on the first court. The bike rack was empty where they got off and parked their bikes. As John and Marlene walked by the first court, the player on the opposite side of the court unloaded on an overhead smash. The ball hit deep in the corner and rattled the fence. If it had gone through it would have hit John. John winced because he was not expecting it.

"Hey, Marlene, how're ya doing? I haven't seen you in awhile. Why haven't you answered my calls?" the dark, muscular tennis player asked.

"I've been busy."

'Who's your friend? Is he some kind of a sissy who only plays tennis with girls?"

*This guy is so arrogant and macho. I would sure like to show him. Who is he to talk to Marlene like that? I would like to show him, John thought.*

"Marlene, is your wimpy friend going to play in the city tournament? I'd like to show him how this game of tennis is supposed to be played. You'll have to find him some other practice partners than girls if he's going to get ready for the tournament."

"Harry, you really think you're so terrific. John will play in the tournament and he isn't afraid to play against you. Why don't you get back to your practicing because you'll need it. There is more to the game of tennis than muscle and mouth," Marlene said with a toss of her head.

John glared at Harry as they walked away.

*What am I going to do now? Marlene thinks I can beat this guy. He hits the ball so hard and is so confident. I would like to show him his place. I hate guys like that. I would give anything in the world to play well against him.*

"Come on, John, we have some practicing to do," Marlene said encouragingly as they walked to the court at the other end of the park.

"Do you believe that I can beat that guy? I would give just about anything if I could."

"I believe you can! Did you say that you would give anything to beat Harry? Well, you can start by first giving up your self-doubt about being able to win," she said as she winked at him. "Now, let's hit some balls!"

Marlene stopped at the entrance to the tennis court and stood quietly, not moving a muscle. Her eyes closed and after a few minutes a soft smile emerged. It was like she was entering a new world. John was getting anxious.

On the court John started out very aggressively, trying to hit the ball with all his strength. Marlene moved effortlessly and returned each stroke. After the ball crossed the net a few times, John would either hit it too long or into the net. He was becoming increasingly irritated and was losing all sense of control.

"Relax, John. You don't need to hit it so hard. I'm not Harry, and you will never beat him playing this way."

"Okay, okay," John snapped back, but he was having difficulty letting go of the anger that he felt toward Harry because of all the demeaning things he had said.

After playing a few more minutes Marlene said, "Let's stop for a while and go for a walk. I need to show you something Mr. Lovano taught me, but first I need to get something from my bike bag."

She was gone only a few minutes and returned with something clutched in her hand. John walked through the gate to meet her, and together they strolled toward the trail in the woods. As they walked, neither of them said anything until Marlene broke the silence.

"Mr. Lovano taught me something which has helped me a great deal. To play my game with greater skill, I had to learn to involve the three different parts of my being -mind, body, and spirit. Everyone has the same problems of how to overcome their feelings caused by doubt and fear due to their lack of faith."

"I'm not even sure what faith is," John said quietly.

"Well, remember that you said, you would give anything to beat Harry, and I said, that you would have to give up your self-doubt?"

"That is easier said than done. Do you have some magical way of doing it?" John asked.

"Yes, and you can call it magical if you want to. Let's find a fire pit in this park. Pick up some small dry sticks. We will need them."

They found a picnic table and a fire pit back in the trees. Marlene took the dry sticks and started a fire with the matches she had been carrying. She also had several small pieces of paper and a pencil.

"John, I want you to sit down and get comfortable. Focus on your breathing. Breath deeply from your stomach. Fill your whole body as you breath in. Hold it for a few seconds and let it out slowly. Concentrate on this for a few minutes. Close your eyes if you wish."

"He felt a bit awkward for a few minutes until he got into the routine. After a few minutes Marlene said, "Think about what you are feeling. Think about Harry and the way he makes you feel. Try to get a vivid image of feeling. In a few moments I am going to give you a piece of paper and a pencil. On the paper I want you to write a word or draw a picture illustrating the feeling. Then on another piece of paper I want you to write a word or symbol of the feeling you would like to have when playing Harry. We will take the first piece of paper and burn it in the fire as you release the feeling, giving it up and affirming that it no longer has a hold on you."

John said quietly, "Can God help me do this?"

"He can if you believe He can. It doesn't hurt to ask."

"As you burn the first piece of paper say, 'I release and let go of my negative thoughts and feelings. I no longer want them to be a part of me. I give thanks for the positive feelings and thoughts which will replace them.'

"Faith allows us to fulfill our commitment to giving up our negative and self destructive thoughts, and in turn helps us to replace them with positive ones. Faith is an act of will. It is a gift of SPIRIT which is strengthened by the power of belief."

John walked over to the fire and lit the edge of the paper. Pausing quietly, he dropped the paper into the fire and walked over to the table and sat down. Sitting there, he seemed to have a different sense about himself. Closing his eyes, he sat very still. After a few moments, Marlene moved over in front of him. Gently, she kissed him on the forehead.

# 8

# MATH OLYMPIAD

"Sometimes our biggest obstacle in accomplishing a goal is overcoming our self-doubt. Our challenge is to change our negative self-image into a positive one by visualizing ourselves succeeding, instead of failing."

Mr. Lovano

John woke up early the next morning to meet with his math teacher and some other students to prepare for the upcoming math competition. The thought of the competition gave him mixed feelings.

*I want to do well in the competition, but I will have difficulty remaining cool and thinking clearly. These feelings -where do they come from? I can't tell if they are from my fear of failure or my desire for success. I just know that I feel on edge when I think about it. I wonder if any of the techniques Mr. Lovano has taught me about channeling my energy on the tennis courts can be applied to preparing for the math competition. Let me think, what were the steps I should take? In my tennis bag is a card he gave me on which the procedure is outlined.*

John found the card in his bag and on it was listed:

## THE STEPS TO SUCCESS

1. Define your goal
2. Write positive affirmations
3. Give thanks for that which you wish to receive
4. Practice mental rehearsal
5. Proceed with an 'I CAN' attitude

Here is the work sheet which he gave me to clarify my objectives. Now, I can take a few minutes to think and meditate on my goal and affirmations for the math competition. Having a little soft background music always helps me to relax and concentrate.

*Well, let me see. My goal is to do very well at the math competition. Now, is that specific enough? Or should I say that I would like to win the math competition for my school. My positive affirmations will be - I enjoy doing math problems. Better yet, I enjoy math challenges. I feel comfortable and relaxed when confronted by math challenges. The joy of competition brings out the best in me. Math is easy for me. Now, I will give thanks to the spirit of truth and wisdom for blessing me with intelligence and confidence.*

Closing his eyes, John took a couple of coins from his pocket and held them in his hands. The room became very still as he went into a moment of deep thought and meditation. After a few minutes a smile appeared on his face and he opened his eyes. A glance at the clock reminded him that he was running short of time. He dropped the coins in a small bank on his dresser and started picking up his things for school.

### FAITH IS BEING SURE OF WHAT WE HOPE FOR AND CERTAIN OF WHAT WE DO NOT SEE.

Hebrews 11:1

"John, you better hurry up if you are going to be in time for the meeting before school," his mother called out from the kitchen.

Swallowing a glass of juice and inhaling his cereal, he headed for the garage to get his bicycle for the ride to school. The air had the fresh cool feeling of a spring day. Riding to school would give him time to reflect and do some mental rehearsal of the events to come. A thought flashed in his mind about the tennis tournament that was to be held later in the month.

*How great it would be to win the tournament! Harry would surely be the one I have to beat. The picture of Harry smashing the ball at him made John feel uncomfortable. HOLD IT, John! right there...and replay that picture in your mind. See Harry smashing the ball, and then see myself making a beautiful return. Remember what Mr. Lovano said, 'It is your imagination, so use it constructively.' I have never put much thought into controlling my thinking until he pointed it out to me. If I don't make an effort to focus on positive things then my mind just sort of runs wild with ideas. Sometimes unconsciously it locks onto negative images which then bring on negative feelings and in turn I can start a downward spiral of self-doubt and that can even lead to depression.*

John had a tennis lesson with Mr. Lovano after school. He was beginning to feel more confident about his strokes, but the real test would be how well he did in the tournament. While he was thinking about the tournament, feelings of stroking the ball well came over him and the vision of hitting a perfect backhand flashed through his mind.

*OH! that feels good. I will play that one over a couple of times in my mind, because I want that one to sink in deep.*

**IF YOU FAIL TO PLANT DESIRES IN YOUR SUBCONSCIOUS MIND IT WILL FEED UPON THE THOUGHTS WHICH REACH IT AS A RESULT OF YOUR NEGLECT**

**Napoleon Hill**

As he pedaled to school his mind was not consciously thinking about riding his bicycle. **HONK! SCREECH!** went the sound of a car horn and skidding of tires. John had unknowlingly ridden through a stop sign. This brought him back to the moment as he turned to avoid the car. The driver was agitated, glaring at him and shaking his head. John waved at the driver and headed down the alley.

*I had better find more appropriate places to do mental rehearsals than while I am riding my bike. I remember Mr. Lovano saying that to achieve one's maximum performance it is necessary to become totally absorbed in the moment and focus all one's energy, mental and physical, on the successful completion of the task at hand. I guess the same can be said about riding bicycles.*

Upon arriving at school John proceeded to his math meeting. The halls were quiet at this time of the morning. That didn't seem quite natural for a school. Mr. Nelson was explaining some problems (or challenges) on the board. John slipped through the doorway and took a seat near the back of the room. Not feeling much interest in the explanation being presented, his mind drifted to thoughts about the upcoming math contest. Images of himself sitting at a table with the other students waiting for the next problem came into clear focus. John could see himself being relaxed and alert. The next problem was read to the contestants. A flash of insight. John raised his hand first and gave the correct answer. He played the whole scene over a couple of times in his mind. John's mind re-focused on the present. Mr. Nelson posed another math problem to the students. A couple of seconds passed and John's hand went up in response.

"John, I didn't know you were part of the living", chuckled Mr. Nelson. "How would you approach this problem?"

"I don't remember the formula to use, but it looks like it can be solved using the Pythagorean theorem," John responded.

"You might have something there. Why don't you come up and show us?"

Walking up to the board John appeared very confident. He showed no hesitation in solving the problem, and acted like he had done it before.

"Well done! That was a more direct approach to solving the problem than I was thinking about," Mr. Nelson said with a surprised look. "You must be putting in some extra time working on your math skills."

"I have just been applying something that I have learned about improving my tennis game to the solving of math problems," John replied.

"I don't know what tennis and math have in common, but I can't argue with results," the teacher commented as the bell rang for first period to begin.

The students filed out of the room. John had a faint smile on his face as he reached the door, and he seemed to be in another world of thought. His next class was in another building. The walk would take him across the campus. Tonight he was to have another tennis lesson with Mr. Lovano. Thoughts of moving around the tennis court making magnificent tennis strokes passed through his mind.

"Hey, Ivan Lendl, where are you going? You must be getting pretty stuck up or are you trying to avoid me?" Marlene said as she closed her locker.

"Oh, sorry, I was just rehearsing hitting my backhand down the line. Here, let me show you my new forehand stroke and follow through."

John swung his arm back as if he had a tennis racket in his hand. While stroking through the shot, his follow through caused his arm to land gently on Marlene's shoulders. She couldn't keep from laughing.

"Did Mr. Lovano teach you that move?"

"No, but if I were to say that I haven't mentally rehearsed it I would be lying," John said coyly. "I need to get in all the practice I can if I am going to do well in the tournament."

"Remember it is a tennis tournament and not a contest on how to figure out thirty different ways to get your arm around a girl," she pointed out. "We'd better hurry to class. How are you and Mr. Lovano doing?

"I have a lesson tonight. I'm feeling more confident and my game is getting more consistent. How about playing tennis with me tomorrow after school?"

"Okay, but I can't get to the courts until 3:30. I have to go home first and get my tennis stuff."

"Great! I'll see you at the courts or should I stop by so we can ride up there together?" John asked.

"Why don't you go straight to the courts so you can save us one? I'll get there as quick as I can. Talk to you later. I don't want to be late for my English class."

# 9

# ANOTHER LESSON

**"The right brain leans toward looking at things negatively and emotionally, while the left is more positive and logical."**

Thomas Blakeslee

Arriving home from school, John quickly changed into his tennis clothes. He picked up the folder Mr. Lovano had made for him which was lying on his desk. Pausing for a minute, he opened the folder. Inside was a holographic picture of a tennis player. When he tilted the picture one way it looked like himself, and moving it another way caused it to look like Ivan Lendl. Moving it quickly back and forth caused the two images to become one. A smile came over his face and he felt confident. Also, inside the folder were pictures of himself hitting beautiful tennis strokes and pictures of his favorite players. He reviewed the page with the statement of his goals and affirmations.

Looking at the digital clock radio on the dresser, he stuffed the folder into his backpack and headed downstairs to get his bicycle. The ride to the courts would give him time to reflect on the pictures of the player he wished to become.

Riding the bike always gave him a feeling of leaving other worries behind. The thoughts and feelings of hitting beautiful tennis strokes began to flow through his mind as he thrust his weight forward into the toe clip on the pedals. Before he realized it, he had reached the steep hill leading to the courts. Intuitively he shifted into the small front sprocket and pulled back on the lever. A familiar grinding sound occurred as the chain slipped onto the lower gear. Another nudge of the lever tuned the chain as he stood up on the pedals and dug into the toe clips.

Before long John reached the crest of the hill and was sitting down on the seat of his bike, riding the last couple of blocks slowly and calmly. The hard exertion climbing the hill cleared his mind.

As John neared the courts, he could see Mr. Lovano on a bench at the end court with his bike parked near him. He was sitting quietly, staring at a tennis ball. John approached him silently, not wanting to interrupt his meditation. After a few moments, Mr. Lovano turned, smiled, and spoke.

"Hi, John. It looks like a great day for tennis! Don't you think so?"

"Yeah, I'm ready!" he responded enthusiastically.

"Before we start some drills, let's go over your folder. This will give me a better understanding of you and your commitment. How do you feel about recording information in it and sharing with me?" asked Mr. Lovano.

"Well, it's okay. At first, I was sort of reluctant to use it, because I didn't want to have to write down my goals. But, once I got into doing it, I think the process helped me to clarify my feelings and increased my commitment. It is kind of spooky at first, being so specific about my goals," John responded quietly.

"Writing one's ideas down helps people to clarify their thoughts. We all need to use devices and procedures which can give form to our creative powers. A person without a positive constructive goal is at best a weak person, at worst an open invitation to negative influences from outside themselves. If you don't set goals in your life, someone else will try to do it for you. I have learned that the lack of direction or goals can breed boredom and lead to depression. A goal encourages us to find the means to express our creativity and exercise our faith," summarized Mr. ovano.

"Maybe that's why, if I have nothing to do, I can really get down on myself. Do you suppose God punishes us for having negative thoughts?" asked John.

"He doesn't have to. We are being punished enough just by harboring negative thoughts. The process of thinking negatively, whether it be out of anger or frustration, just takes us farther away from a state of grace in which we feel in tune with a higher spiritual power. We have the ability to choose what we think about if we will take a few minutes to reflect on the phenomenon of thinking. Thoughts evoke emotions which bring on other thoughts and emotions that can start a downward spiral to despair and depression. To feel in tune with our higher self, we need to divert our attention toward hope and away from fear. For example, on the tennis court if you are waiting to return a serve fearing that your opponent will serve to your backhand, the thought of fear will inhibit your ability to make an effective return because you are projecting to

Attention Directed
Toward Hope . . .

. . . And Away from
Fear & Self Doubt

Higher Self

Hope Evaluates

Lower Self

Fear brings us down
and defeats us.

Fig. 14

your subconscious a picture of yourself missing a shot. If your thoughts were positive and you were looking forward to returning a serve from the backhand side, you would project the image and feelings of a perfect backhand return. We need to realize that our imagination is a stronger force than our will. If you're consciously thinking, 'I need to make a good return,' but visually imagining hitting long or into the net, your body will respond to the visual image in your imagination. Therefore, it is important to focus on that which you want to happen and not on what you don't want to happen. It is hard to motivate yourself with the reverse of an idea, like 'Don't hit it long.' Your ability to play well will depend on whether you can keep your attention focused on what you wish to accomplish.

## YOUR SUBCONSCIOUS MIND CANNOT REMAIN IDLE.

## IF YOU FAIL TO PLANT DESIRES IN YOUR SUBCONSCIOUS MIND IT WILL FEED UPON THE THOUGHTS WHICH REACH IT AS A RESULT OF YOUR NEGLECT.

Napoleon Hill

"Would you review my goals with me to see how they could be better stated, Mr. Lovano?"

"Let's look at them" said Mr. Lovano.

**1. Win my division in the tennis tournament.**

**2. Beat Harry in the tournament!**

**3. Become the best tennis player I am capable of being.**

"Well, the first and third goals seem to be well stated. The focus of your effort should be on number three, the other two may happen as a result. Revenge and anger are strong motivators but they won't help you play with calmness or confidence. You can't beat Harry anyway, because he is on the other side of the net and you're not allowed to strike another player. Besides, errors outnumber great shots twenty to one at the intermediate level of playing which means Harry will beat himself if you give him a chance. Therefore, your goal should be to return every ball hit to you to the best of your ability. Your opponent is not the adversary, but rather someone who offers you the opportunity to play at a higher level of competence. Fear and self-doubt are the true adversaries. Your goal should be to align your mind, body, and spirit in an effort to become totally absorbed in the activity of playing tennis. When you get into the flow, winning and losing will no longer mean anything. Your ego will cease to exist and you will feel like you have reached a state of perfection."

## HUMAN BEINGS HAVE BEEN, AND REMAIN, UNIQUELY CREATIVE BECAUSE THEY ARE ABLE TO INTEGRATE THE PESSIMISM OF INTELLIGENCE WITH THE OPTIMISM OF WILL

Dr. Robert Schueler

"I think I understand what you are saying. If I begin to think only of winning or losing, my game will start to fall apart, even if I have a large lead. If I think too much about the score and start playing tentatively before I know what's happening, I am choking and might lose the set. What should I think about?" questioned John.

"Hitting beautiful shots. Imagine yourself playing like your favorite tennis player. You have to raise your self-image to a level of play equal to or greater than that of your opponent. If you have made a number of mistakes, the tendency would be to identify with your mistakes. It is human nature for us to be negative and identify with the past. It doesn't have to be so. Refusing to let the past drag you down is often going against the intellect, which is more inclined to be swayed by factual information, but it can be done! Projecting yourself to higher levels of play is an act of will and faith. To dare to go beyond past accomplishments takes mental rehearsal. People who have excelled beyond their peers use their imagination creatively. Joe Namath, a famous football player, was asked how he became a great quarterback. He said that he had a coach who told him if he wanted to accomplish something he should dream about it first. The point is - **IT'S YOUR IMAGINATION - TAKE CONTROL OF IT.** How we react under pressure or stress is pretty much determined by what is programmed into our subconscious. The subconscious mind is more receptive to information when the body is relaxed; that is why I encourage you to use the audio tapes before going to sleep or when you take a few minutes to relax. You will program your mind with positive affirmations when you are receptive. Achievement in athletics is over fifty percent mental. Studies in sports psychology have shown that athletes who divide their time between mental exercise and physical exercise out perform those who spend all their time on physical exercise," said Mr. Lovano.

"Okay, how I can use this process to win the tennis tournament? I will probably have to play Harry, who has very powerful strokes. He really crunches the ball on the serve and it is really fast and hard. How can I prepare for that?" John asked.

## EXERCISE
## BODY AND MIND

## TO EXCEL "BALANCE"
## YOUR PHYSICAL EXERCISE
## WITH YOUR MENTAL EXERCISE

Fig. 15

"Observe his playing. Make a good visual image of how he tosses the ball and how he takes his racket back and leans into the stroke. Notice where the ball bounces and how it bounces. Then, when you have a good visual picture of him playing, place yourself mentally on the other side of the court, making perfect returns with lots of confidence. Go over this situation many times in your mind. Whenever you have a few moments replay this thought as vividly as possible.

"In an interview, Chris Evert was asked how she practiced for a championship match. She stated that, in addition to actual practice, she carefully and painstakingly tended to rehearse every significant detail of an upcoming match in her mind's eye. She would think about her opponent's style and form, and visualize herself countering each and every maneuver that person might make during the match. Providing the mind with a preview of an upcoming event does a great deal to sidetrack negative thoughts and feelings."

"But Mr. Lovano, is there anything I can do on the tennis court to get rid of fear and anxiety? Sometimes I can tell I am beginning to feel fearful and my confidence is leaving. I'm choking and I know it, but can't seem to do anything about it. What can I do to stop this?" John asked.

"There are a couple of things you can do. First, slow down. Play more deliberately. You are allowed 30 seconds between each point and 60 seconds between each game. Use some of that time to compose yourself. Second, focus on your breathing. Exhale and breathe deeply into your abdomen. Remember the breathing exercise on the audio tape for mental rehearsal. Say to yourself as you exhale: 'I breathe out fear and anxiety.' As you inhale, say: 'I breathe in confidence and energy.' Remember, this can also be practiced off the court, since in the heat of competition your thoughts can become confused. The tendency for a person who is becoming fearful is to stoop his shoulders forward. His breathing becomes more shallow, decreasing the amount of oxygen to the brain and increasing the anxiety," stressed Mr. Lovano.

"What about some of the things I learned using the biofeedback?" interjected John.

"Good point, John! Consciously relax your forehead as you do in the float game. Think about controlling the balloons and letting them drift downward. Get the Ken Rosewall look. Look with 'soft eyes' relaxing the eyebrows. Like this!" Mr. Lovano said as he relaxed his eyebrows and slightly closed his eyes. "It will help your eyes focus on the ball. A tennis match is a lesson in stress management. Once you learn some of the tools to control anxiety it will help you in other parts of your life. Make an affirmation to yourself."

### I AM CALM; I AM RELAXED!

# 10

# MARLENE'S GIFT

**"The whole business of living is to fulfill yourself, to enhance your sense of self-respect. When you do this, you express the God-like quality within you."**

Maxwell Maltz

The afternoon air was warm and the sky was a soft shade of blue. It was a perfect day for tennis. John had hurried home from school, raided the refrigerator, changed clothes, grabbed his tennis racket, and was riding to the tennis court before anyone at home realized he had ever been there. Marlene had said she would be twenty minutes late and he should get there early in case they had to wait in line for a tennis court. Speeding along on his bike like an Olympic athlete in a time trial, he seemed to be driven by a power from another level of consciousness.

John wondered about the special gift Marlene said she had for him. She was hard to figure out. She seemed to have so much depth to her personality, like a complex work of art. She had taught him a lot about how to strengthen his confidence on the tennis court. He was beginning to feel like he had a chance to win the tournament. It would make him feel great to win and his parents would be so proud. He'd just have to stay confident. He started to wonder. What if he didn't do well at all? He caught his thought and deliberately said out loud, "Don't let your mind feed on the negative thoughts." He remembered the words of Mr. Lovano, "If you let your thoughts dwell on the negative, you give them the soil and nutrients for them to grow. Discard them like weeds. Pull them out! Plant positive thoughts and affirmations."

**"I WILL DO WELL!"** he said out loud.

The tennis courts came into view as he rounded the corner. It appeared that not all of the courts were in use. The last two courts were, in fact, empty. Stopping his bike by the park bench, he rested one foot on the wooden seat to balance himself as he looked at his watch. Three fifteen; he still had some time before Marlene would arrive. Taking a can of balls from his backpack, with a racket in hand, he opened the gate to the court. This extra time would be good for practicing his serve. He took four balls and built a small pyramid in the deuce court near the center line. Taking the rest of the balls, he walked over to the other side of the court and positioned himself to serve. After a few practice swings he started serving. His first serves were erratic, but the fifth missed by only a couple of feet. Walking over to retrieve the balls he started thinking.

*I have seen Mr. Lovano hit the pyramid of balls at least one in ten tries and most of his shots came very close. I wonder how he does it? I know, by positive thinking and visualization. When I get back to the other side I'll practice visualizing my ball rocketing into the pile of balls and sending them in every direction, an explosion of yellow balls. I can see it happening in my mind's eye. I'll run that image through my mind again. BOOM! There they go again. ple of balls. Close, but a little short. A little wide. I must stop le of balls. Now I'll serve a couand visualize again. Another close one. Two more tries before I have to go pick up the balls again. Another close one. Correct a little to the left. I know I can do this. I will close my eyes and visualize once more. I feel myself making the swing and contacting the ball. Every part of my body is synchronized. I feel confident. Becoming one with the ball! Here it goes. Looks good! On target. ALL RIGHT! I DID IT!*

"Hey, **GREAT SHOT JOHN!**" Marlene yelled from the park bench near his bike. He had been so engrossed in his meditation on hitting the pile of tennis balls that he had not seen her arrive. As he walked toward her he noticed a package in her lap wrapped in blue paper.

"I didn't see you ride up."

"You were concentrating so hard I didn't want to disturb you. How many tries did it take you?" Marlene asked.

"Let me see. I guess it was my tenth try."

"Great, then you win the prize. I have this present I want you to open."

John took the package and shook it. It didn't rattle. Eagerly but carefully he took off the blue paper and opened the box. Inside the box was a light blue T-shirt. A drawing of a can with an eye on it was on the front side and on the back it said, **I AM, THEREFORE I CAN.**

"That's an interesting design on the front. What's it mean? Eye on a can. Oh yeah! I CAN. Where did you get this shirt?" questioned John.

"From Mr. Lovano. Who else?"

"I'll wear it while we practice. It probably has some magical powers! Are you ready to hit? I'll be pretty awesome with this T-shirt on."

**I AM
THEREFORE
I CAN**

Fig. 16

"Sure, I think I can handle you!"

Marlene picked up her racket and walked to the gate. She stopped and stood still, not saying anything for what seemed like minutes. With a quiet smile she entered the court.

"Was something wrong? Or were you meditating?"

"Just doing something Mr. Lovano encouraged me to do. He calls it 'a moment of transition.' I have found it quite helpful."

"What do you do? May I ask?"

"Before I go onto the tennis court, I take a few moments to visualize myself hitting beautiful strokes. Then I give a prayer of thanks for all the beautiful shots I am going to make. God is omnipresent, always there, and in all things. The prayer of thanks helps me to be aware of my spiritual dimension and helps me to rid my mind of fear and self-doubt. Besides, it makes me feel better to know I am not alone on the court. I feel more confident from having taken this quiet reflective moment."

"I think I'm beginning to understand. Positive thinking goes beyond wanting to do something and saying, I can do it. I must practice doing it in my mind's eye and reinforcing it with a prayer of thanks. The leap of faith takes us from 'I want to' to 'I know I can.' Faith is the foundation on which the temple of confidence is built. I have the choice either to believe in myself and my abilities or not to believe in them. Someone else can try to do it for me, but if it is to last and face the test of competition, I've got to take charge of how I believe in myself. Thanks for the gifts, Marlene," John said as he hugged her.

# 11

# TOURNAMENT

"Confidence is built off the court. Imagination provides the bricks and faith is the mortar."

Mr. Lovano

The weekend of the tournament had finally arrived. John played well his first two rounds, winning in straight sets. The semi-final match had tested him, since it had gone to three sets. The game scores were 6-3, 4-6, 7-5. It is the second day of the tournament and Harry is playing his semi-final match.

"Marlene, please save my seat. I want to go over to the end of the court and visualize what it is like to return Harry's serve."

John walked to the end of the court and thought.

Harry's serve has a lot of speed behind it, but it doesn't have much variety. If I shorten my back-swing and meet it solidly my return will have a lot of pace on it. Whenever he serves a flat serve his toss is always out in front. Yes, I can picture it, hitting a beautiful backhand return to his feet. He hits a weak short volley. **BAM!!** I hit a passing shot by him. **GREAT**, I think I'll play that one through my mind again. Now, he's serving into the ad court. Down the middle to my forehand. No problem. A little more time to hit a strong return. The ball looks as big as a basketball. I can see the seams as it rotates. Drive this one deep and down the middle. Harry hits a cross-court forehand drive. I get to it easily and send it back deep. His return is short. While moving to the net, I hit a deep approach shot to his backhand. He tries to drive it past me. I anticipate it and block the volley to the opposite side for a winner. Great shot, John.

"'Hey kid! Watch out! The way you are swinging your arms you almost spilled my coffee," cautioned a man walking by.

"Oh, sorry. Just practicing my return of serve."

"Oh, yes, now I recognize you. You're the one who will be playing in the finals against the winner of this match. Looks like you'll have your hands full. He's a lot bigger than you and really hits the ball hard. I wish you the best of luck."

"Thanks."

*I'm not counting on luck. I'm working on faith. Luck is what you start looking for when your faith and confidence have weakened. I am the sculptor of my spirit, chipping away and discarding my negative thoughts and feelings in order to allow the positive ones to dominate my attitude.*

*Harry is really working this guy over. He seems to be getting intimidated by Harry's serve and volley game. I'll spend some more time tonight visualizing returning Harry's serve. It appears he will have more trouble hitting a strong volley on the forehand side if I keep the ball low to the net on the return. I think I will go talk to Mr. Lovano. He is scouting the match using his computer and the COMPU-TENNIS program. After the match we'll go over the printout.*

"John, have you noticed that when Harry gets on a roll he starts speeding up the game? This really frustrates his opponent. Tomorrow you don't have to let him hurry you. Slow down and be more deliberate in your actions. Take time to regain your composure. Remember, you have 30 seconds between points," Mr. Lovano said.

"Have you noticed anything in particular about Harry's game?"

"His serve is hard and flat, but does not have much variety. He just hits it as hard as he can."

"I noticed that too. I am going back over to sit with Marlene and I'll talk to you after the match. I'll have a lot of time to work on my mental game since the match is not until tomorrow."

"Make sure you concentrate on watching the match," Mr. Lovano said with a smile as John left.

The match did not last a long time. The final score was 6-1, 6-2. This meant that John and Harry would play the final the next afternoon. The weather forecast was for hot and sunny conditions. After the match, John and Marlene went for a walk.

"I'm not sure I can beat this guy. He really has a powerful game. He hits the ball a lot harder than I do," commented John.

"Hey, come on! I'm not giving up on you, so don't give up on yourself. You have plenty of time to get yourself mentally ready for this match. Between now and the match tomorrow you'll have plenty of time to mentally rehearse playing your best tennis against Harry. Remember, don't use your creative imagination negatively and rehearse failure. You don't have to overpower him. Just keep hitting the ball back and increase amount of time it takes to play each point. Don't let Harry's aura intimidate you. I know you can beat him. He is only human. In fact, he will beat himself if you keep the ball in play. I'll help you practice your lobs. He will be coming to the net a lot, and he will want to get the points and match over quickly."

"Okay, I know what you're saying but I have never been in the finals of a tournament. I'm playing out of my comfort zone."

"Let's find a quiet place where we can work on your self-image. We can go for a walk up the trail behind the courts."

"You're not going to let me give up mentally before the match, are you?"

"No way! I think you are a winner, so you had better begin to think like a winner. Here is a good place to work on your mental game. Sit down and get yourself comfortable. There, that's good. Now, close your eyes and focus on your breathing. Let the outside world melt away. Let go of any negative feelings you have about your ability. Say to yourself, 'I release and let go of these feelings; I no longer need them. Breathe in confidence. Breathe out fear and anxiety. 'I am a child of God. Only my thoughts can hurt me and only if I let them. I release and let go of any thoughts of fear and self-doubt. I am a being of infinite energy. I will hit every ball with grace and power. I will not give up. Giving up is not part of my nature. I love to play point after point. I do not limit myself by thinking limited thoughts.

"Visualize yourself out on the tennis court. Harry is on the other side of the net. See yourself hitting beautiful returns. Let the feelings of the strokes flow through your body. You feel confident and relaxed."

"Hold it, Marlene! Are you trying to hypnotize me again?" John broke in.

"Sure, if that is what it takes for you to believe in yourself. It is one thing to intellectually think you are a great tennis player, but it won't do you any good unless you emotionally feel that you are a great tennis player. We need to get the feeling part of you involved and get beyond the ego which wants to stay in control. A person has to move from, 'I want to be good at something' to 'I believe I am good at it.' Visualization helps us see ourselves succeeding, but it takes a leap of faith to get you to the next step. Since you couldn't make the leap of faith by yourself, I was using guided imagery to help you see yourself succeeding. What we need to bring about in you is a feeling of supreme confidence. Having the will to try your best, no matter how great the obstacle, is what the match is about. The match tomorrow doesn't have to be a contest where one wins and the other loses. The most meaningful contest is within yourself, whether you can maintain your resolve to do your best. You may win or lose the match, but you will always be a winner if you have conquered your negative thinking and feelings."

The most meaningful
Contest is with yourself.

Fig. 17

# 12

## FINALS

*"In life and in sports what matters most is not whether you win or lose, but how you play the game."*

author unknown

"Thirty, Forty. Advantage to Mr. Harry Monzer," the umpire called from the chair.

The score in the first set is 4-4. John is serving and behind in the score. The sun is directly overhead and both players are dripping with sweat. Bleachers have been put on both sides of the court and only a few seats are empty.

*I've got to win this point. Otherwise, Harry will be ahead 5-4 and serving for the set. I'll hit a hard flat one down the middle. Take your time, John. Toss the ball out in front of you. Lean into it. BAM! GOOD SERVE! Right where I wanted it to go. Oh, no. He was waiting for it. His return is coming hard and low at my feet. Should have come in on this one. Forehand volley. MOVE! Weak volley. Trouble. He's moving in on it and going to hit a winner down the line. There it goes. No chance to get it. DAMN! NOW I am behind 4-5 and he starts serving. John, you've got to turn this set around. It's time to change ends of the court. I have a few minutes to think.*

Now, playing his serve and volley game, Harry is forcing John to play defensively. The next serve is an ace down the middle. John, playing with more resolve, keeps getting the ball back. The points are getting longer and longer as the ball travels back and forth over the net. John wins one and loses the other. Behind 40-30, John needs the next point to stay in the set. Harry's serve is wide to the backhand, but John counters with a deep return to the opposite corner of the court. Caught off guard, Harry's return is short. John moves in to make a deep approach shot to the forehand corner. Harry makes a wild swing. The ball hits the net. Forty-all. With an extra reserve of strength the next two points go to Harry. He hits another ace down the middle and serves and volleys for the next point in order to win the set.

Walking to the chairs at the net John sits down. Putting his head in his towel he doesn't move for a long time. He reaches into his tennis bag to get something to drink and his hand finds a soft drink can with a piece of paper wrapped around it. On the paper was the picture of a human eye.

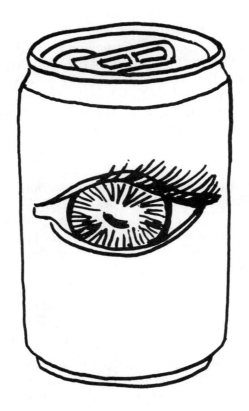

Fig. 18

*EYE CAN. I CAN. They're at it again. I know who is behind this. Marlene probably put this in my bag knowing I might need to get my positive mental attitude back. What the heck? Whether I am confident or fearful depends upon the thoughts I dwell on. I am going to hang in there this next set. Harry might think he has broken my spirit after the last set. Well, I'm not beaten yet. I won't give up. The next set I will be serving first.*

Mixing up his serves, John wins the first game of the second set. Both players are serving well. The points are getting longer. Because his power game requires more strength, Harry is losing some of his edge. After forty-five minutes into the second set the score is tied at six games each. A twelve point tie-breaker needs to be played. Serving first, John hits a spin serve to the backhand. His opponent, being in too much of a hurry, miss-times his return. The ball goes wide. Harry is to serve the next two points.

*I have to hit a good return. NO, restate that, John. I love to hit beautiful returns. Losers think I HAVE TO. Winners think I WANT TO. I WILL. Be positive. Visualize a beautiful return. Focus on the ball. Observe the spin. I feel confident and full of energy. Up on your toes. He is tossing the ball up. **BACKHAND RETURN.** Hit through the ball. Deep. Felt good. **FOREHAND.** Go for it. Return deep and down the middle. He is returning to my backhand and moving in. Top spin lob over him. Follow through. Good shot.*

John starts off leading the tie-breaker 2-0. Harry comes back with a serve-volley combination, then wins the next point with an overhead smash. Both players trade points back and forth until score of the game is tied 6-6. Since the score is tied, the play is continued until a player wins by two points. The players change ends of the court and John will serve.

*Six-all. It's on the line now. Slow down, John! Your opponent is just as much or more anxious than you are. Play deliberately. Say an affirmation. 'I love the excitement of playing tie-breakers. There is no other place that I would like to be than here and now.' Hit the spin serve to his backhand. On target. The return is deep down the middle.*

*Drive the ball back down the middle. Watch for an opening. His return is going to be a little short on my forehand side. Under-spin the ball to his backhand corner and move up. Good, it is deep enough. He is going to hit it down the line. Reach out and punch through it. GREAT SHOT! THE SET IS MINE.*

The match score is one set each. The third set is to be played after a short break. John looks over at the stands and can see his father and mother, Marlene, and Mr. Lovano all sitting together. Marlene is looking back at him, holds up her clinched fist, and shakes it with excitement. When play resumes Harry will be serving first.

The crowd cheers as the players return to the court for the final set. Harry is determined to finish this match once and for all, as he is back in his old form with his good serve and volley game. Before John knows what is happening the first game is over. John comes back and wins his serve, but with more finesse than strength. The third game goes again to Harry. In the fourth game Harry makes some beautiful returns of John's serves that catch him off guard. This rattles John and he makes two double faults and loses the game, 3-1. The players then trade games back and forth until the score is 5-3. John has to break Harry's serve in order to stay in the match.

*I am behind now, but there is no need to panic. Play one point at a time. Visualize yourself hitting beautiful returns. Think positively. If Harry continues to hit hard flat serves, then shorten your back-swing and return them low over the center of the net as he is moving in. Think about what you want to happen and don't focus on what you don't want to happen. My mind will cause my body to reproduce the actions based on the images I have been imagining. See yourself succeeding.*

Harry is now serving to win the match point, but he is acting a little over-confident. He hesitates before coming in and is caught off guard by a ball hit along the sideline. The score is 30-40, John leading. Harry serves a hard deep shot which skips off the line, then moves in for the kill. John's return is low over the center of the net, but Harry volleys it deep into the backhand corner. Out of desperation John sends up a high lob into the sun. Harry backs up, but is having trouble finding the ball in the sun. He hesitates and then swings. The ball lands a foot out. Game score is 5-4. John holds his serve to even the score at five all. Each player wins his next serve to make it 6-6 which sets up another tie-breaker. The umpire opens a new can of balls and gives them to Harry. The new balls are faster and his first serve is a bullet down the middle. John barely gets his racket on the ball and is unable to return it. As the ball hits the net, John stands still for a moment, then restrokes the return, going through the motions as if he has returned it perfectly. Before serving, he turns and looks up at the sun as if to absorb energy from it. The crowd is quiet. Both players are dripping sweat from the hot day.

*The sun is energy sent from above. I accept this gift from above as it renews my strength and desire. I enjoy playing tie-breakers. There is no other place I would like to be than right here and now. I have been serving spin serves all day and he is expecting them. Let's hit a flat one down the center to keep him honest. BAM! On target. Just as if I were aiming toward the stack of balls during a practice. He was not expecting it. Weak shot return. Move up. Volley deep cross court. It worked. Score tied 1-1.*

The points are traded back and forth. At 7-7, Harry serves. The ball hits the backhand corner and John sends back a good deep return. The ball crosses the net many times. John's next return is a little short. Harry drives it deep and advances to the net. Anticipating his opponent's move, John drives it down the line to win the point. The noise of the crowd fills the air. "Advantage to Mr. John Brasky," calls the umpire. As the noise of the crowd dies, John turns to the sun again, standing still while he looks up. The sun shines brightly on his sweat-drenched forehead and a half smile is on his face. One more point and his dreams can come true. Standing impatiently at the service line, Harry is eager to even the score. The crowd becomes quiet. **BAM!** The serve is hit straight at John. Moving to the right he blocks the return back, but it is a short return. Harry moves in and returns it deep to the backhand corner. Having no choice, John hits a high deep lob into the sun. Moving back, Harry hesitates and then unloads all his strength on the ball. John runs back. With a quick flick of the wrist, he slaps at the ball. His return hits the top of the net and hangs there for a moment before falling into Harry's side of the court. A loud cheer erupts from the crowd.

A quiet smile appears on John's face as he strolls to the net. The match is over and he has won.

*Harry put up a good fight. The match could have gone either way. Harry is a good competitor and a worthy opponent, but today I am blessed with a double victory. One on the outside with Harry and the other on the inside with myself. And really, now that I think about it, I will always be a winner when I have mastered my inner game. The greater victory has been over myself, to derail my thoughts of fear, self-doubt, and negative thinking, as well as for me to play with tireless faith and savor every moment of the struggle.*

"Good match Harry. It could have gone either way!"

"Thanks, you were lucky today, but you also played well," Harry responds as they shook hands.

*John thinks to himself, maybe there was a little luck. Luck or faith, which is the deciding factor? Well anyway, I prefer to believe it was faith.*

# EPILOGUE

JOHN REFLECTED OVER HIS PROCESS OF BECOMING A WINNER. HE REALIZED HOW HE HAD LEARNED TO OVERCOME FEAR, ANXIETY, AND SELF-DOUBT. SINCE THIS WAS A VALUABLE LESSON, HE MADE A COMMITMENT TO TEACH THE PROCESS TO OTHERS.

## WHAT JOHN HAS GAINED AND DESIRES TO SHARE WITH OTHERS.

1. Winners think like winners with positive affirmations and self-talk.
2. Winners see themselves winning by using visual imagery in order to rehearse successful experiences.
3. Winners set goals and make commitments to their goals. They are motivated by their desire to achieve.
4. Winners back their desire for success with faith, knowing that they must replace their fear with faith.
5. Winners understand the principles of the creative power of thought. Thoughts held in mind produce results after their kind. Whatever the mind can conceive and believe, it can achieve.
6. Winners can manage their emotions. They use their emotions positively and constructively to help them to achieve the results they desire.
7. Winners give 100 percent of their attention to whatever they are doing.
8. Winners think positively because they know that negative thoughts produce negative energy.
9. Winners know that the toughest opponent is themselves, and once they have learned the process of self-mastery they can handle whatever challenge life has to offer.
10. Winners wish to share their success and they desire to share the secrets for success with others.
11. Winners are on a quest to understand the meaning of God.

# RECOMMENDED READINGS

**BOOKS**

Bennett, James G. and Pravitz, James E. THE MIRACLE OF SPORTS PSYCHOLOGY. Englewood Cliffs, New Jersey: Prentice Hall, Inc. 1982

Frankl, Victor E. MAN'S SEARCH FOR MEANING. New York:Washington Square Press, Inc. 1963

Glasser, William. TAKE EFFECTIVE CONTROL OF YOUR LIFE. New York: Harper & Row. 1984

Gawain, Shakti. CREATIVE VISUALIZATION. Mill Valley, California: Whatever Publishing. 1978

Garfield, Charles A. PEAK PERFORMANCE. Warner Books. Los Angeles, Ca. 1984

Karlins, Marvin and Andrews, Lewis M. BIO-FEEDBACK, New York: Warner Paperback Library. 1973

Kiersy, David and Bates, Marilyn. PLEASE UNDERSTAND ME. (Character & Temperament Types). Del Mar, Ca: Prometheus Nameis Book Co. 1984

Lazarus, Arnold. IN A MIND'S EYE. Rawson Associates Publishers, Inc. New York 1978

Loehr, James E. MENTAL TOUGHNESS TRAINING FOR SPORTS, The Stephen Greene Press, Lexington, Massachusetts 1986

McGinnis, Alan Loy. BRING OUT THE BEST IN PEOPLE. Augsburg Publishing House. Minneapolis. 1986

Millman, Dan. THE WARRIOR ATHLETE. Stillpoint Publishing, New Hempshire. 1979

Moe, David E. OPENING HEARTS AND MINDS. Moe-Tavation Unlimited, Issaquah, Wa 1986

Ostrander, Sheila and Lynn Schroeder. SUPERLEARNING, New York: Delacorte/ Confucian Press, 1979

Peale, Norman Vincent. DYNAMIC IMAGING. Old Tappan, New Jersey:Fleming H. Revell Company. 1982

Russell, Peter. THE BRAIN BOOK. E. P. Dutton, Inc. New York 1979

Weinberg, Robert S. THE MENTAL ADVANTAGE. Leisure Press. Champaign, Illinois 1988

Waitley, Denis. THE DOUBLE WIN. Old Tappan, New Jersey: Flemming H. Revell Company. 1985

## COMPUTER PROGRAMS

LEARNING STYLE ANALYZER, Moe-tavation Unlimited. Issaquah, Wa. 1985

PERSONALITY ANALYZER, Psycom Software. Cincinnati, Ohio. 1984

RELAX, Synapse Software Corporation. Richmond, Ca. 1984

## SUGGESTED LISTENING

Bandrowski, Jim and Curry, Hayden. THE MENTAL GAME. Med-A-Tape Company. Waco, Texas. 1979

Braden, Vic. SINGLES STRATEGY SECRETS. Success Motivation Cassettes, Inc. Waco Texas. 1982

Bristol, Claude M. THE MAGIC OF BELIEVING. Success Motivation Cassettes, Inc. Waco Texas. 1982

Hill, Napoleon. THINK AND GROW RICH, Success Motivation Cassettes, Inc. Waco Texas. 1982

Meyer, Paul J. THE POWER OF GOAL SETTING. Success Motivation International, Inc. Waco, Texas. 1982

Moe, David E. MAXIMIZING YOUR POTENTIAL, Moe- Tavation Unlimited. Issaquah, Wa. 1985

Sweetland, Ben. I CAN - THE KEY TO LIFE'S GOLDEN SECRETS, Success Motivation Cassettes. Waco, Texas. 1960

Waitley, Denis. THE PSYCHOLOGY OF WINNING. Nightingale and Conant Corp. Chicago, Illinois. 1982

For more information:
David E. Moe
12900 246th S.E.
Issaquah, WA 98027

# NOTES

# MR. LOVANO at his best....again
## OTHER BOOKS BY DAVID E. MOE

### OPENING HEARTS AND MINDS

An inspiring, straightforward book that answers the questions: What really motivates people? Why are some people more motivated than others? How do you get people to motivate themselves? How do we stimulate others to learn the secrets of motivation? Parents, teachers, students — AND YOU — will benefit from reading this book. Parents, teachers, and other readers of OPENING

HEARTS AND MINDS will be impressed with Mr. Lovano's use of guided imagery, educational charades, motivational psychology, and computers to break through to his students. In the process of doing so, the author, through Lovano, offers many practical ideas for use in everyday life — and demonstrates how and why some people are more successful than others.

"If every teacher would be like Mr. Lovano in this book, every child would feel worthy and would be able and want to learn everything. Mr. Lovano, the ideal teacher, shows his students that he really cares about each one. He teaches them to relax and be receptive by means of biofeedback, relaxation meditations etc. He uses computers, students helping each other and his own personal encouragement of each student. A book for every teacher and every parent."

*-Margot Curtis--Unity Book Store Newsletter*

"A most enjoyable and refreshing book to read - I like the format."

*-Marge Goetz, B.S.--Social Worker*

"Thought-provoking - every parent should read it."

*-Ed Hogenauer--parent*

"I read it with pleasure - and I trust that you'll find many eager readers."

*-Henry Maier--Retired Professor of Social Work University of Washington*

"Your book (OPENING HEARTS AND MINDS) really excited me and touched my heart."

*-Jim Trudowski--Associate Professor Carrol of Montana - College*

"Just bought and finished (four times) your book, OPENING HEARTS AND MINDS. It made me feel good...and hopeful...and lots of my kids seemed to enjoy reading through it also.

*-Patty Helm--teacher , Lummi Island, Wa*

"I whole heartedly agree with your philosophy expressed in the book."

*-Elaine Caldwell--Parent Educator El Rancho Adult School Pico Rivera, Ca*

# ABOUT THE AUTHOR

David Moe is a teacher, philosopher, counselor, mathematician, and tennis player. In an effort to improve his own game of tennis he did research in sports psychology, theology, and learning theory. The results of his studies improved his own games and life as well as provided him with information to help others.

Dave's book the *The Making of a Winner* originated with his experiences as a tennis player, coach, and counselor. It is a book dealing with understanding ourselves, that should motivate not only tennis players and coaches, but anyone who wishes to become a better person. It might challenge some basic beliefs about learning and being. Nevertheless, the story transcends mere "learning techniques", because it answers basic questions about how we learn and what motivates each of us.

Mr. Lovano, the main character in the story, is more than a coach and teacher; he is a transformer, who blends together on the tennis court the wisdom of past and present generations to show how the ideas complement each other. His techniques and modern ideas - using a computer as an assessment tool - help his students make quantum leaps in attitude modification so they can become successful tennis players and better people.

# YES, I WOULD LIKE TO ORDER MORE BOOKS

**Winning Ways Press**  12900 246th S. E.  Issaquah, WA  98027

**OPENING HEARTS AND MINDS** by David E. Moe  $7.95
**THE MAKING OF A WINNER** by David E. Moe  $7.95

_____

Name

I have enclosed:

Personal check ☐

_____

Address

VISA ☐   MasterCard ☐

_____

City

Card Number

_____

_____

State

Expiration Date

_____

Signature

_____

Zip

_____

| | UNIT | QTY. | TOTAL |
|---|---|---|---|
| **Opening Hearts and Minds** | $7.95 | | |
| **The Making of a Winner** | $7.95 | | |
| Subtotal | | | |
| Shipping charge (first book) | $2.00 | | |
| Shipping each additional book | $ .50 | | |
| Washington state residents add 8.1% sales tax | | | |
| **TOTAL** | | | |